Curious Canadians

Nancy Liss & Ted Liss

Fitzhenry & Whiteside

Curious Canadians © 2002 Fitzhenry & Whiteside

To our family and friends for their encouragement and support.

Fitzhenry & Whiteside Limited
195 Allstate Parkway
Markham, Ontario L3R 4T8

www.fitzhenry.ca godwit@fitzhenry

Fitzhenry & Whiteside acknowledges with thanks the Canada Council for the
Arts, the Government of Canada through its Book Publishing Industry
Development Program, and the Ontario Arts Council for their support of our
publishing program.

10 9 8 7 6 5 4 3 2 1

National Library of Canada Cataloguing in Publication Data

Liss, Nancy
        Curious Canadians

Includes index.
ISBN 1-55041-412-7

1. Canada—Biography. 2. Canada—History. I. Liss, Ted II. Title.

FC25.L57 2002   971'.009'9   C2002-901704-9
F1005.L57 2002

Printed and bound in Canada
Cover and textual design: Karen Petherick, Markham, Ontario

Contents

Acknowledgements   vii

Introduction   ix

Part One: Dreamers

The Many Lives of Father Goose   3

A Vision in a Bottle   11

Castle in the Wilderness   18

Against All Odds   24

Little Ship on the Prairie   29

Henry Hoet's Obsession   35

Part Two: Schemers

The Last Laugh   43

The Great Groundhog Caper   48

Sam Kee's Revenge   54

Lost Lemon Mine   58

A Pain Named Butt   66

They Called It Little Chicago   70

Brother Twelve   78

Part Three: Finders, Seekers

From the Amazon to the Arctic   87

The Mushrow Astrolabes   96

Wild Bill Peyto   103

Tilikum Voyage   109

In Pursuit of Treasure   116

Part Four: A Different Kind of Hero

Four Funerals For Sophia Cameron	127
Above and Beyond the Call of Duty	136
Godmother to the West	141
The Mightiest Man in the World	148
Titanic Lifeboat Number 6	154
The Great Farini	162

Part Five: A Question of Identity

Doctor Barry's Secret	173
The Real Story of Grey Owl	180
A Soldier in Disguise	190
The Strange Case of Susannah Buckler	197
Whose Coffin Is It Anyway?	202

Part Six: Strange and Mysterious

Gone Without a Trace	211
Falsely Accused	217
The Dark Side of the Island	225
The Phantom Train Disaster	229
The Loss of the Fairy Queen	235
Bibliography	241
Photo Credits	247
Index	249

Acknowledgements

We wish to express our deepest gratitude to the following people and organizations for their valuable contributions to this book. Special thanks to the many librarians, researchers, curators and archivists for their expertise and interest in our project. This book would not have been possible without their help. If we have inadvertently forgotten any names, we offer our humble apologies and our sincere appreciation.

The Ontario Arts Council; Bill Lishman, Blackstock, ON; Eldon and Diane Johnson, Boswell, BC; Elinor Barr, Thunder Bay, ON; Arlene and Ed Flickinger, Cardston, AB; Laurene Shaw Sabey, Calgary, AB; Ross Murray, Shediac, NB; James Masters, Owen Sound, ON; Don Starkell, Winnipeg, MB; Jeff Starkell, Mississauga, ON; Wayne Mushrow, Port aux Basques, NF; Henry and Elizabeth Gibbons, Port aux Basques, NF; Dan Blankenship, Oak Island, NS; Iris Smith, Broadview, SK; Cora MacKenzie, Fortune Bridge, PEI; Mabel MacLean, Summerstown, ON; David Anderson, Williamstown, ON; Ralph Getson, Lunenburg, NS; Beulah Allen, Lunenburg, NS; Jane Tanner, Lunenburg, NS; Bea Renton, Lunenburg, NS; Mayor Lawrence Mawhinney, Lunenburg, NS; Alan Millar, Toronto, ON; Yaletown Productions, Vancouver, BC; Vancouver Public Library, Vancouver, BC; Vancouver City Archives, Vancouver, BC; City of Victoria Archives, Victoria, BC; Thunder Bay Historical Museum Society, Thunder Bay, ON; The Gulf Museum, Port aux Basques, NF; Ignace Public Library, Ignace, ON; St. Martin's in the Woods Church, Shediac, NB; Mormon Temple of Cardston, AB; Toronto Reference Library, Toronto, ON; Owen Sound *Sun-Times*, Owen Sound, ON; Chinese Cultural Centre, Vancouver, BC; Glenbow

Museum and Archives, Calgary, AB; Provincial Archives of Alberta, Edmonton, AB; Moose Jaw Public Library and Archives, Moose Jaw, SK; Tunnels of Little Chicago, Moose Jaw, SK; Sukanen Pioneer Village and Museum, Moose Jaw, SK; Whyte Museum of the Canadian Rockies, Banff, AB; Maritime Museum, Victoria, BC; British Columbia Archives, Victoria, BC; Broadview Museum, Broadview, SK; St. Boniface Museum, St. Boniface, MB; City of Toronto Archives, Toronto, ON; Archives of Ontario, Toronto, ON; Port Hope Public Library, Port Hope, ON; Wellcome Trust Medical Photographic Library, London, England; National Archives of Canada, Ottawa, ON; Saskatchewan Archives Board, Saskatoon, SK; Clarke Historical Library, Central Michigan University, Mt. Pleasant, MI; Barkerville Museum, Barkerville, BC; PEI Public Archives, Charlottetown, PEI; Public Archives of Nova Scotia, Halifax, NS; Lunenburg *Progress-Enterprise*, Lunenburg, NS; Toronto Historical Society, Toronto, ON; Medicine Hat Museum and Art Gallery Archives; Kirk of St. James, Charlottetown, PEI; New Brunswick Museum, Saint John, NB.

Introduction

The writing of *Curious Canadians* had as many unexpected twists and turns as some of the stories in our collection. Naturally curious and eager to explore, we wanted to know more about Canada and its people. What began as a collection of unsolved Canadian mysteries soon developed a life of its own and grew into something much, much bigger.

There were two major turning points in this process. The first occurred in Lunenburg, Nova Scotia, with the discovery of Sophia McLaughlin, a young girl who was falsely accused and subsequently died of a broken heart. Something about her story touched us so deeply that we had to write about it. We felt then, as we do now, that this story of a town righting a wrong after so many years is a Canadian classic.

Our second turning point came a few years later in Barkerville, British Columbia, a living museum depicting life during the gold rush. It was there that we found the gravesite of Cariboo Cameron, a different kind of hero. Being hopeless romantics ourselves, we were overwhelmed by what this extraordinary man did in the name of love.

There were other truly unique personalities we came across in the course of our research, whose passion and dedication were nothing short of inspirational. Ed Bunyan, the editor of the *North Bay Nugget*, comes to mind. This remarkable man knew the true identity of Grey Owl but sat on the story for three long years, because he would not allow Grey Owl's important work to be undermined by a media scandal. We knew that our book would have to encompass all of these wonderful stories.

So for seven years we crisscrossed the country, meeting all sorts of interesting people and gathering information along the way. When we began our travels, we had no idea where our research would ultimately lead us, but we were committed to accuracy no matter how long it took us to uncover the facts.

Our pursuit led us to some rather unexpected places. The first trip, from Toronto to Newfoundland, was our honeymoon. How many newlyweds can say they spent their honeymoon in libraries, archives and cemeteries? We soon discovered that tombstones have stories of their own to tell and are often excellent sources of information.

Of course, nothing can compare with the excitement of meeting our curious Canadians in person, like the colourful Wayne Mushrow, a diver who found a priceless artifact in Newfoundland waters. Not only did Wayne share his amazing story with us, he gave us a priceless gift that he made—an exact replica of his discovery carved out of wood, complete with all the ancient markings. And then there's Bill Lishman, a one-of-a-kind if ever we met one. Bill is the original Father Goose and was the subject of a major Hollywood movie, *Fly Away Home*. We were thrilled when Bill invited us to see his remarkable underground home and to share his many schemes and dreams with us over a cup of coffee. And the list goes on.

Curious Canadians represents over 60,000 kilometres of driving, through everything from fog so thick we couldn't see our hood ornament, snow so high it buried the highway signs, floods that washed out the Trans Canada Highway, and a shower of yellow grasshoppers that covered the car. We even drove right through a tornado. City slickers that we are, we had many "interesting" encounters with moose, elk, deer, bears and a persistent mountain sheep that kept trying to get into the car with us.

Curious Canadians provided us with many unique and memorable moments. We discovered that Canada is filled with a host of extraordinary characters past and present—lovable eccentrics, fascinating adventurers, bizarre schemers and many who dared to be different and follow their dreams. The most gratifying part of producing this book however, would have to be meeting so many wonderful people during our travels. Their interest, enthusiasm and willingness to share their stories was heart-warming.

For us, this is just the beginning. What started as a hobby has turned into a vocation. We know there are many more stories just waiting to be discovered. As Alice said in Wonderland, "Curiouser and curiouser!"

Happy reading.

Nancy and Ted

Part One

Dreamers

The Many Lives
of Father Goose

FOR MOST OF US, FANTASIES ARE THE STUFF OF HOPES AND DREAMS. For Bill Lishman, the famous sculptor who taught a flock of wild geese to fly behind his ultralight plane, fantasies are simply projects he hasn't gotten around to yet. Artist, sculptor, architect, inventor, designer, author, film-maker, stuntman, naturalist and entrepreneur, Bill Lishman has done it all.

Father Goose, Bill Lishman.

His well-documented adventures with Canada geese excited the imagination of Hollywood and in 1996 a fictionalized version of his life was brought to the big screen. The movie, *Fly Away Home*, directed by Carroll Ballard and starring Jeff Daniels, featured Lishman as Daniels's double. Lishman did all of Daniels's flying stunts on his original Easy Riser and acted as technical consultant for the film.

Despite this impressive list of achievements, the road to success was a bumpy one for Bill Lishman. School was painfully difficult for him as a young boy. Back in the days of his rural one-room schoolhouse, no one had ever heard of dyslexia, and young Bill, labelled a slow learner, was forced to repeat grade one. As a youngster, Lishman's hopes of obtaining a pilot's licence came to an end when he joined the Royal Canadian Air Cadets in Oshawa. The frail, short and skinny 13-year-old managed to pass the ground school, but failed the test for colour blindness.

Lishman became a rebellious teenager with a reputation as a troublemaker in school. After several unsuccessful academic ventures, he attended the Ontario College of Art, but left before completing his first year, despite achieving the college's highest mark in sculpture.

In 1966 the restless sculptor headed south to Mexico. It was in the mountain town of San Miguel de Allende that his life took a dramatic turn when he met a Canadian girl who was studying Mexican textile arts. Paula Vockeroth, a statuesque beauty, was only 17 at the time. Bill and Paula lived together in Mexico, then returned to Paula's parents in a north Toronto suburb, announcing their wedding plans. The Vockeroths were shocked. They had sent their daughter away to broaden her education, never dreaming she would return with a 27-year-old, unemployed hippy artist. Lishman, however, was determined—and in love. The couple married the following year and have been a solid team ever since, sharing in each other's ventures and pursuits. Son-in-law Bill has long since gained the respect and affection of Paula's parents.

Lishman's artistic career began to attract serious attention when he orchestrated one of the cleverest publicity stunts in history. With only six dollars' worth of scrap metal, Bill Lishman created a large welded steel horse. Now he needed a way to promote his sculpture. Inspired by the legend of the Trojan Horse, Lishman and a friend deposited the massive statue in front of Toronto City Hall in the middle of the night. By the next morning it had created a sensation. No one knew where the statue had come from or who had ordered it. City Hall bureaucrats were bewildered and security was thrown into turmoil. The press loved it. Bill's Trojan horse made the front pages of all the newspapers and the story was covered extensively on national television. Eventually word got out that the statue was a Lishman creation. The horse ended up being shown at the 1967 Royal Winter Fair. Prince Philip opened the national agriculture and livestock exhibition that year and publicly praised the statue. Bill sold many horses as a result of the publicity.

Neil Armstrong's lunar landing in 1969 had a profound impact on Lishman. He decided that he, too, had to have a lunar lander. It took two and a half years to build (and film) an exact replica of the lunar module which he called *Moonship on Earth.* Lishman's film was aired in both Canada and the U.S. during the final lunar landing of Apollo 17 in December of 1972. Lishman assumed his module would be snapped up by some trendy, eager buyer, but it sat on a side road near his home for 12 years. Always ready for a good prank, Lishman rigged the module with lights and scattered scorched grass around it, making it look as if the module had recently landed. Passersby would stop and stare, often slamming on their brakes to take a second look. Lishman's *Moonship* eventually found a buyer and was donated to the Oklahoma Aviation and Space Hall of Fame in 1983 in honour of the 25th anniversary of NASA.

In 1986, Chrysler Corporation hired Lishman to create a catchy, promotional statue for its Plymouth Sundance and Dodge Shadow. Lishman constructed a perfect, full-scale replica of Britain's Stonehenge using crushed cars. The famous landscape sculpture—*Autohenge*—has appeared in photographs all over the world. Many of Lishman's works can be seen in parks, fairs and expositions around the globe. His 26-metre human tower, *Transcending the Traffic*, became one of the centrepieces of Expo '86 in Vancouver.

Lishman is also an accomplished filmmaker and author. His landmark 3-D IMAX film, *The Last Buffalo*, directed by Stephen Low, is a standard opening feature at 3-D IMAX theatres worldwide. His book, *Father Goose*, was published in Canada and the U.S. in 1995 by Little, Brown & Co. (Canada) Ltd.

While Bill's career has been moving forward, Paula Lishman has been creating masterpieces of her own. With her expertise in textile arts, she devised an original technique for making a fur yarn. By weaving or knitting this yarn, she produced a remarkably light, warm fabric with fur on both sides. Together the Lishmans developed a highly successful fashion business. Her fur garments have been seen on runways from Milan and New York to Tokyo. In the early years, Paula modelled her own designs while Bill acted as fashion photographer. Several of his photos of Paula appeared in Vogue magazine. Paula Lishman's fur fabric creations have grown into a Canadian success story, employing 180 people and boasting gross annual sales reaching $10 million. In 1995, Paula was chosen Woman Entrepreneur of the Year in the category of International Competitiveness. Bill Lishman is an executive of the company. In fact, it was the profits from their lucrative business that made Lishman's claim to fame as Father Goose possible.

Lishman had always dreamed of flying with the birds. In 1985 his friend Bill Carrick, a naturalist and filmmaker, was involved in the making of an IMAX film called *Skyward*, in which he trained 30 Canada geese to fly with a boat. Carrick supplied Lishman with goose eggs and coached him on early bird behaviour based on the experimental research of Austrian scientist, Konrad Lorenz. Lorenz discovered that young birds become attached to the first thing they see after they hatch in a process called imprinting. When Carrick's goslings hatched, the first things they saw were Lishman and Carrick, so the two instantly became surrogate parents.

Raising the geese became a family affair involving Lishman's children, Aaron, Geordie and Carmen. Lishman would get up at 6:30 every morning to take the goslings for a run, teaching them to follow him. As they ran, he carried a tape recorder hanging from a pouch, and played the goslings the sounds of the ultralight motor to get them used to moving to the sound of his aircraft.

Bill Lishman in his goose look-alike ultralight with friends.

The ultralight, another Lishman design, is a highly modified hang glider with clear wings, an engine and propeller. At first Lishman had to experiment to find the right flight speed for his goose-children. One day, after many mishaps and frustrations, he looked behind his airborne craft and saw the geese trying to catch up. Lishman was fascinated by their fluid movements and says the word "flapping" in no way describes the graceful air ballet of their flight. He realized that the geese fly in the famous V-formation in order to conserve energy. The lead goose works the hardest. Each successive goose has an easier and easier time as it rides the air wave created by the goose ahead of it. The V-formation constantly changes with a new leader taking over when the first becomes tired. The birds continue the process down the chain so the work is shared.

In 1993 Bill Lishman, photographer/pilot Joseph Duff, and Dr. William Sladen of Virginia teamed up to put Lishman's imprinting experiments to practical use. In October, Lishman and Duff taught a flock of Canada geese a new migration route. In large waterfowl, migration is not instinctive. It is a learned behaviour that young geese acquire from their parents—in this case, Lishman and Duff. Flying in two ultralight aircraft, they led a flock of geese 650 kilometres from Ontario to the Yawkey Center, a wildlife preserve at Airlie, near Warrenton, Virginia.

Lishman's ultimate goal was to see the geese return to his (and their) Ontario home, thereby establishing a true migration route. On December 13 Lishman and Duff packed up to drive home. Two days after their departure, the entire flock vanished. Christmas came and went, but still no geese. The birds were expected to return home by early spring. By mid-April everyone's spirits were at an all-time low. Lishman and Duff were searching for the flock in the U.S. when they received an unexpected call from Paula that the geese had arrived back home in Ontario. It was the publicity surrounding this wild goose chase the eventually led to the making of *Fly Away Home*.

It is only fitting that a family as unconventional as the Lishmans should live in an unconventional house. Bill Lishman, who spends so much of his time soaring above the ground, enjoys living beneath it. The 250 square metre Hobbit House, as it is affectionately called, consists of seven onion-shaped domes like interconnected igloos, built underground. From the air, the house looks like a hill with barnacles.

The idea came to Lishman one very windy day as he was standing on the hill of his rural Ontario property near Lake Scugog. He thought it might make more sense to live below ground than above it. Construction of the high-tech home began immediately. It became a once-in-a-lifetime experience for the contractors working on the project. The top of Purple Hill was taken off, the domes were put in and then the earth was returned, restoring the hill again. Midway through construction, a building inspector came to look over the project. He left scratching his head, saying, "What do I know?"

Entrance to the Lishman subterranean home. Note the skylights on the grass roof.

Surprisingly, the rooms are all bathed in light from the skylights in the "ceiling." There is plenty of living space, with no square-cornered rooms anywhere in the house. Even Lishman's refrigerator, his own invention, is in perfect keeping with the theme of the house. Not your typical icebox design, the Lishman fridge is a buried cylinder concealed within the lower kitchen cabinet. Press a button under the counter and watch it pop up like a giant thermos bottle, perfectly insulated. When asked why the house was never used in *Fly Away Home*, Lishman explains that the executives of the movie were afraid no one would believe it.

Lishman always liked the feeling of living in a cave and feels that his cozy, environmentally friendly residence will last forever. Because of the dome construction, it is as structurally strong as an egg. It can take the pressure of the surrounding earth, so the concrete walls are only about 6 centimetres thick. Since the house is situated below the frost line, there is only a 10-degree difference in temperature between winter and summer.

Lishman finds the domes spiritually uplifting, like a cathedral. He says people are not rectangular, so why put them into rectangular architecture? According to Lishman, people feel more at home in an environment that reflects the roundness and curves of the human body. His rooms contain soft beanbag chairs, comfortable curved furnishings and a tubular metal Lishman Rocker. There is enough space for physical activity of all kinds, including a climbing wall and a trapeze in the main room. The acoustics are excellent; two small speakers are enough to fill the room with music. Trying to detect where the sound of a cricket is coming from, however, can be maddening.

Life-size self-portrait in metal.

Lishman's geese return every spring to Lake Scugog and Purple Hill. They seem to have no trouble locating their surrogate parents buried underground. For visitors using more human forms of transportation, directions might be necessary. Just turn left at the big blue camel, along the statue-lined driveway, and look for someone mowing the roof.

A Vision
In A Bottle

TELL ANYONE ABOUT DAVID BROWN AND HIS FAMOUS
HOUSE IN BOSWELL ON THE ROCKY SHORES OF
KOOTENAY LAKE, B.C., AND THEY ARE BOUND TO USE
THE WORDS "WEIRD," "ECCENTRIC," AND "MORBID." But
visitors who have actually seen David Brown's house are sur-
prised beyond their wildest dreams.

*The Glass House, Boswell, BC., a fully modern six-room home
constructed entirely of 500,000 455 ml glass embalming bottles.*

Weird maybe, eccentric certainly, but this fairytale glass castle is undeniably beautiful and elegant with its glass bridges, archways, turrets, winding pathway and miniature lighthouse. David Brown claimed that he created his house "to indulge a whim of a peculiar nature." How did he come up with such an extraordinary idea?

Growing up during the Great Depression, young David quickly learned the value of a dollar. Nothing around the Brown home was casually thrown away. Everyday items were cleverly re-used and recycled. Brown remembered these lessons well. His practical background combined with an artist's imagination and a sense of humour, inspired him to create British Columbia's most environmentally unique retirement home—a home made of 500,000 empty embalming fluid bottles.

David Brown was born in Ontario but moved with his parents to Vegreville, Alberta, as a youngster. The family ran a funeral business that eventually expanded to Lacombe and Red Deer. For 35 years David Brown worked as a funeral director in the small communities of rural Alberta. Stories eventually began circulating that Mr. Brown was seen nodding off unexpectedly on the job, which proved awkward for a man of his profession. Brown's doctor suggested that perhaps it was time to retire and David Brown left the funeral business at the age of 52 to save his health.

He hitched a 4-metre trailer to his car and travelled west to build his dream home. Brown had a vision of a quiet retirement home overlooking the peace and tranquility of beautiful Kootenay Lake in the mountains of British Columbia. In fact, his vision was so clear that he was able to describe precise details of the house to his wife. Mrs. Brown listened carefully and surprised him with an oil painting that bore a remarkable likeness to the real thing long before it was completed.

For years, funeral homes threw away their empty embalming fluid bottles. Not David Brown. With the ingenious eye of an artist, he came to realize that he had the perfect building block right in his hands. The old 16-ounce (455 ml) glass bottles

Distinguished portrait of David Brown, funeral director.

could be used as bricks. Now came the daunting task of collecting enough of them to build a house.

Brown took a part-time job selling embalming fluid to funeral homes from Victoria, B.C., to Thunder Bay, Ontario. His contacts in the funeral profession knew they would never have to worry about what to do with all their empty glass bottles. Brown was only too happy to make the rounds in his pickup truck delivering embalming fluid and picking up about 2,000 empties per trip. Finally in 1952, when he had collected enough to get started, Brown quit his job and began to build, driving around the country collecting more empties as he needed them.

David Brown, planner and architect, building his recycled dream home.

It took two years of hard, dedicated work to cement 400 bottles a day by hand. In the evening, after checking to see that all the cracks in the cement were properly filled, Brown watered each new section, making sure the cement cured slowly. The following morning, using only a round wire disc on the end of an electric drill, each bottle was individually polished until it sparkled like a jewel in the sun. Then he would cement another 400 bottles and repeat the same process, slowly working his way through the gigantic pile of empty embalming fluid bottles piled on his property.

When the house was nearly finished, the Browns were able to move out of their trailer. The family was looking forward to the peace and quiet of their new home. And what a home it was—111 square metres of living space built in a cloverleaf pattern with three circular main rooms and a foyer. The walls were one bottle in thickness with the bottoms facing the outside and the bottlenecks pointing inward. The electrical wiring was threaded around the necks. Strips of wood were fitted between the necks and cemented in place for strength and stability, allowing for cedar boards to be used to form the inside walls. Beautiful leaded glass windows looked out onto a glass and stone walled terrace overlooking Kootenay Lake.

From the start, the house attracted a lot of attention. Word soon spread and people began to drop by to take a look. Everyone thought Brown's home was some kind of joke. It got to the point where the family could not finish a meal without someone peeking in the windows. Brown remembered what an old minister back in Vegreville, Alberta, had once told him. "One way to break up a congregation is to start

It was estimated that the bottles provided the insulation value equivalent to 70 cm of fibreglass.

passing the donation plate." Brown thought if he began charging admission to see the house, maybe the curiosity seekers would go away. Wrong. Before long the family was forced to hire staff to admit people, answer their endless questions and take them on tour.

David Brown could often be found walking about his property, working in his garden or selling tickets. People assumed he was just one of the staff, never dreaming that this was the man who had created the masterpiece they were admiring. When asked, he would playfully tell them that David Brown was reading on the terrace or working inside the house if they wanted to talk to him. Of course when they got there, they discovered that David Brown was the one who had sold them the ticket.

Folks who knew David Brown as a funeral director in Red Deer, Alberta, were well aware of his creative, artistic side. In his early days Brown had been a drummer, creating sound effects for silent movies. He often played in the theatre in Red Deer or performed as a magician, doing shows for the local Lions Club. Still, folks were amazed when they saw the glass house. Over the years, Brown had told many of them about his dream but few really expected him to accomplish his goal. Obviously they underestimated their friend's determination and stamina to complete such a massive recycling project.

In fact, David Brown was a remarkable planner and architect. He had little formal training in construction, yet his house is structurally sound and offers superb insulation. Architectural consultants from Austin, Texas, estimated that the air trapped inside the bottles provides the equivalent of over 70 centimetres of fibreglass batting. The fireplace with its 900-kilogram rock mantel is all that is needed to heat the interior, and the house remains comfortably cool all summer. In addition, the experts agreed that the location of the house, perched on solid granite outcroppings, provided the perfect support for the tremendous weight of it all—a staggering 454 tonnes of glass and cement. To date, over half a million glass bottles have been used for the house and all additional structures on the property.

David Brown died on July 13, 1970, at the age of 70. Mrs. Brown, son Eldon and his wife Diane live in the house and operate it as a tourist attraction from May to October. The family is continuing Brown's work by adding extra features to the property. Numerous lawn ornaments are found among the flowers and carefully landscaped lawn. The family continues to operate a refreshment stand and gift shop, welcoming tourists to the glass house.

To this day there are several visitors who remember David Brown with great affection and kindness. They tell the family that he was the one who buried their mother or father years ago, and now they have returned to show their grandchildren the house. Others have heard about the glass house through tourist information centres in the area and had to see it for themselves. They ask the same questions that were asked 40 years ago. Eldon has heard it all before. Many are surprised to find that some of the bottles still contain slight traces of embalming fluid in a variety of different colours. Eldon casually explains that different chemicals were used for different purposes. He laughs at the notion of the house being considered morbid, and reminds people who live in wood houses that caskets are made of wood.

From May to October a steady stream of cars stops by the house. When November rolls around, the family can finally relax and enjoy David Brown's labour of love—a quiet retirement home overlooking the peace and tranquility of beautiful Kootenay Lake in the mountains of British Columbia.

Castle in the
Wilderness

**IN THE HEART OF NORTHWESTERN ONTARIO'S WILDER-
NESS, A MOST UNUSUAL BUILDING RISES AS PART OF
THE LANDSCAPE.** Situated on the shores of White Otter Lake,
an imposing log castle has been the source of mystery and
romance for over 80 years.

The famous log Castle at White Otter Lake.

The nearest town, Ignace, is about 50 kilometres away by plane or, for the more adventurous, an ambitious canoe trip with 18 difficult portages. In the winter Ignace can only be reached by snowmobile, yet isolated as it is, the Castle continues to attract thousands of visitors. People are fascinated by the unusual 3-storey structure and adjoining tower, built single-handedly by one man over a period of 17 years. The Castle is massive, yet Jimmy McOuat, its creator, was a surprisingly slim, wiry, white-haired man in his fifties, standing no more than 170 centimetres.

He has been labelled in folklore as the Hermit of White Otter Lake, an immigrant and an eccentric. Much that has been written about McOuat is false. Even his name has been misspelled and mispronounced so often that he is more commonly known as Jimmy McQuat than McOuat (pronounced Ma-Cue-itt).

In 1914 a journalist visited Jimmy at his remote log castle and published an article entitled "The Hermit of White Otter Lake." From then on, Jimmy jokingly referred to himself as "the Hermit" though he was known to be a gracious host and a friendly, frequent visitor to Ignace.

It has been said that Jimmy McOuat immigrated from Scotland and that he left behind a Scottish sweetheart for whom he built the castle. Sadly, the story goes, the girl was of noble birth and at the last moment, changed her mind about living the common life. She never came, never saw the magnificent home he had built for her, and broke Jimmy's heart. A touching tale, but fictitious.

Elinor Barr, author and local historian, discounts these rumours, claiming that many of the fabrications were designed to enhance the mystique and romance of the Castle and to promote tourism in the area. It was her father, fire ranger Tony Berglund, who discovered Jimmy McOuat's body and buried him by his famous log castle. After extensive research, Elinor Barr was able to separate the facts from the fiction and has set the record straight.

*Hoping to attract
a mail-order bride,
Jimmy McOuat provided
this portrait.*

James Alexander McOuat was born in 1855, the youngest of six sons. The first McOuats came to Canada from Scotland to work as stonemasons on Ottawa's Rideau Canal. They settled in the Brownsburg area of the Ottawa Valley north of Montreal.

At the age of 31, Jimmy McOuat boarded Canada's first transcontinental train and headed west, choosing a homestead of 45 hectares near Emo, Ontario. He began to clear the land and build a small cabin for himself, but he was lonely. Most of the local women were already married. He asked a neighbour who was travelling east to fetch him a mail-order bride from southern Ontario. Jimmy gave his neighbour a portrait of himself and a letter in which he described his intentions:

"I use no liquor nor tobacco, nor do I make use of profane language ... I have not much learning but I have morality and character to make up. I would like a girl under 27 years, not too thundering big, brought up on a farm ... Her hair may be any colour but fiery red ... Please oblige your neighbour, Jas. A. McOuat."

Surprisingly, a young lady agreed to the match. Nineteen-year-old Jane Gibson was bright, attractive and a good homemaker. Her only stipulation was that Jimmy come east to meet her family. At the last minute, however, Jimmy declined and young Jane married another suitor. Perhaps this is how the story that he built the Castle for a long lost love got started.

Jimmy then began to get involved in the community. The confirmed bachelor became secretary-treasurer of the local school board. He worked hard, and by 1898 McOuat had accumulated enough money to buy two neighbouring farms. Jimmy was a success but it was not destined to last. By 1900 he had sold his farms and turned to prospecting, but within two years the mines closed. The little gold rush ended as quickly as it began and Jimmy McOuat lost his entire life savings.

In 1903, with no money or property, Jimmy found a spot on White Otter Lake and settled there. He built a crude log shack and became a trapper—the only resident to live in the area year-round. Life in the remote reaches of wilderness was not easy. Jimmy lived an isolated, solitary existence. All the while, he was haunted by a silly boyhood curse that inspired him to change his life.

When asked why he built his fantastic log castle on White Otter Lake, Jimmy recalled an event from his childhood. He and a buddy were playing together. As a prank, his friend threw a cob of corn at a man, hitting him in the ear. Not knowing who had thrown the corn, the man assumed it was Jimmy. He began cursing the boy, saying, "Jimmy McOuat, ye'll never do any good—ye'll die in a shack." Young Jimmy was too loyal a friend to set the record straight and stood there nervously as the man continued his outburst.

While living in the little shack on the shores of White Otter Lake, Jimmy McOuat constantly thought about the curse and was determined to prove it wrong. He kept thinking "I must build me a house." And so he did, in grand wilderness style.

The Castle, complete with a lookout tower, was constructed out of the giant red pines growing near his shack. Some weighed nearly 900 kg. Oldtimers claimed that the glass for his windows (all 26 of them) came in ready-made sashes which he brought in by canoe from Ignace, carrying the load over 18 portages. By 1914 the walls and the roof of the Castle were completed. McOuat somehow managed to haul the logs with a homemade hand winch, hoist them and then hold them in place while he carefully dovetailed the ends for an air-tight seal. Jimmy McOuat was 59 at the time. For about 17 years he worked tirelessly on his own. Finally when the Castle was completed, Jimmy applied for title to the land on which his masterpiece stood. He was refused, although the Department of Lands and Forests accepted his cash deposit and gave him a receipt.

Despite this setback, Jimmy continued to fish, plant vegetables and bake his own bread. In his spare time he surrounded the Castle with flowers. During the First World War, he sent the Battalion leaving Fort Francis a huge box filled with flowers, and offered the Castle as a convalescent home for wounded soldiers. To make things more comfortable for the veterans, he installed a heating system and fully furnished the building.

Three years after his first request for title to his land, McOuat wrote again to the Lands Department. This time they considered his request and asked for more information. Jimmy never had a chance to reply. In October of 1918 while netting fish not far from his home, he became entangled in his nets. Jimmy was dragged into the water and drowned. The following summer, fire rangers scouting the area discovered his decomposing body. They buried him in a coffin made from lumber he had sawn himself. The Castle became his headstone.

For nearly 70 years the empty Castle faced the elements, as well as the vandals who took everything from windows to lumber and furnishings. At one point the Ministry of Natural Resources thought about having the structure demolished since restoring it was considered too costly. If not for the determination of the Friends of White Otter Castle, a group of concerned citizens from Ignace and Atikokan, the Castle might have been destroyed. Ignace adopted the Castle as a civic symbol. Today Jimmy McOuat's Castle is one of the biggest tourist sites in the Dryden District—a monument to the pioneer spirit and one man's dream.

Against All Odds

ON THE NORTHERN COAST OF NEW BRUNSWICK LIES THE POPULAR SUMMERTIME RESORT OF SHEDIAC. Famous for its warm beaches, Shediac is also known as the lobster capital of the world. Most of the residents in this area can trace their ancestry back to their French-Acadian roots, but the first European settler was actually a young Englishman named William Hannington, who settled in Shediac because of a misunderstanding.

In March of 1785 Hannington left England for Nova Scotia to take possession of a large tract of land which he had purchased sight unseen for £500. The 2,024 hectare property was supposedly a day's walk from Halifax—or so Hannington was led to believe. It was not until he arrived that he learned it was nearly 300 kilometres away in New Brunswick.

William Hannington was a strong-willed, determined man. Not easily discouraged, he decided to make the long overland journey to find the exact location of the land he had come to settle. With Mr. Roberts, a companion whom he had met en route, and a native Mi'kmaq guide, William Hannington set out with all his worldly goods piled on a sled and headed for Shediac. The long trek through the freezing cold snow of March was more than the two Englishmen had anticipated. They spent several nights shivering in the bitter cold under shelters made of tree boughs that their guide had put together.

The men finally reached their destination, only to face the desolate sight of Hannington's property. It was covered in a dense forest of huge pine trees embedded in deep layers of snow. This disappointment was more than Mr. Roberts could bear. He returned to Halifax where he booked passage on the first ship back to England.

Hannington, however, saw potential in the wilderness and chose to remain. He settled in a small log cabin on his land. It wasn't long before he became friendly with his Aboriginal neighbours. Together they lived and traded in harmony, establishing a successful trading partnership. Before long, Hannington became quite prosperous. In addition to his successful ventures in trading, he began to increase his wealth by selling the lumber he cleared from his land to other settlers who came to the area.

Within a few years, William Hannington was able to build himself an impressive 3-storey frame house. It was a rather large home for a bachelor living alone in the wilderness. Hannington felt that he had reached a point in his life where he required a wife and heirs to share in his good fortune. He had heard stories of English-speaking settlers living on Prince Edward Island, known then as the Island of St. John. Since there were no available young ladies living in the Shediac area, it seemed like an ideal place to find himself a bride. And so in 1792, after being alone for seven years, Hannington hired two Mi'kmaq guides to take him across Northumberland Strait to the island by birch bark canoe.

While riding along a dirt road on the island in a borrowed ox cart, Hannington caught a glimpse of a young lady, Mary Derby, feeding some chickens. Without a moment's hesitation, he jumped off the ox cart, approached the young maiden and proposed marriage to her. Fortunately Mary was not the kind of girl who required a lengthy courtship. She accepted immediately. Since no clergymen were available, the couple climbed into the ox cart together and made their way to a nearby Justice of the Peace where they were married on the spot. After a quick farewell to Mary's family, the newlyweds hopped into the canoe and were soon on their way to Hannington's home at Shediac.

Together the Hanningtons worked and prospered, establishing not only themselves, but the town as well. The marriage proved to be a fruitful one, producing 13 children of whom 12 survived. Religion played an important role in the Hanningtons' lives. Services were held every Sunday in their Shediac home, attended by friends and neighbours. Hannington founded a Sunday School library and the local church that he called St. Martin's-in-the-Woods, after St.-Martin's-in-the-Field, his beloved church back home in England.

In 1831 William Hannington suffered a stroke. He died seven years later at the age of 79 and was buried in the church-yard of St. Martin's-in-the-Woods. A magnificent monument was erected in his memory. The massive stone structure had to be hauled by six horses a dis-tance of 60 kilometres to his gravesite. It was beauti-fully designed and sculpted by skilled artisans at a cost of £100—a considerable sum of money back then. The top of the monument was made of a large solid block of stone supported by four stone pillars.

St. Martin's-in-the-Woods, Shediac, NB.

A memorial inscription describing the contributions of Hannington, Shediac's most honoured citizen, was carved into the slabs of stone.

Over the years the cemetery at St. Martin's-in-the-Woods became overgrown and neglected. Weeds and moss covered the

Massive monument to William Hannington, found in the cemetery of St. Martin's-in-the-Woods. Note the mysterious missing piece under the top edge.

gravesites and monuments, hiding their inscriptions and concealing their intricate artistry and carvings. A century after Hannington's death, workmen were hired to clean up the grounds and restore the ancient monuments.

While working on the massive top of Hannington's grave, two workers noticed something suspicious. Loose particles crumbled away from the underside of the stone slab revealing a panel about 30 centimetres wide, tightly wedged underneath the stone top. With great effort, the workers managed to loosen the panel and slide it out like a drawer. Inside the panel they found what appeared to be a chart or map describing the location of a treasure at "the place of disembarkment." Specific directions indicating the exact number of paces and turns were included in the note.

The workmen were locals and immediately concluded that the "place of disembarkment" referred to Shediac Island, where they knew many early settlers had disembarked. In total secrecy, they went to the island and began digging, refusing to tell anyone about the secret panel in the tombstone or the discovery of the note. Naturally, a secret of this magnitude could not be kept quiet for long. In no time the island was overrun by fortune hunters in a frantic race to unearth the treasure, but after numerous attempts, no treasure was ever reported to be found.

Today William Hannington's tombstone stands as an important piece of monumental art, but many questions remain unanswered about the secret panel. Was there ever really a treasure or was the treasure map simply a hoax? Whatever the answer, the mystery has managed to rekindle an interest in this dynamic man who established a town out of the wilderness.

Little Ship
on the Prairie

**THEY SAID HE WAS MAD—THAT IT COULDN'T BE DONE—
BUT TOM SUKANEN PAID LITTLE ATTENTION TO THE
RUMOURS AND GOSSIP CIRCULATING AROUND TOWN. HE
HAD A VISION AND NOTHING WOULD STOP HIM.** Today his
ship of dreams is one of the strangest sights in the Canadian
West, sitting landlocked in the middle of the Prairies 1,600
kilometres from the nearest sea. This is Tom Sukanen's story.

*Portrait of Tom Sukanen, on the Prairies, taken with his own self-
made camera.*

On October 29, 1929, the stock market crashed, ushering in the Great Depression. Then a devastating drought left the Prairies parched and vulnerable to howling winds, turning the landscape into dust. Crops were ruined, topsoil literally blew away and desperation set in. Many homesteaders were forced to abandon farms that had been in their families for generations. Tom Sukanen seemed oblivious to the misfortune and hardship around him. In the midst of the "Dirty Thirties," he began spending a veritable fortune on a bizarre scheme.

His impoverished neighbours had plenty to talk about when a huge shipment of expensive building supplies appeared on Sukanen's property. To many, the "crazy Finn" had always seemed a little eccentric, living in a silo-shaped house topped by a revolving periscope from which he kept a suspicious eye on his surroundings. They were used to his unusual inventions but this latest shipment of goods appeared to border on madness.

Tom Sukanen was born Tomi Jaanus Alankola in Finland on September 23, 1878. By the turn of the century, economic conditions in Finland prompted many desperate Finns to seek greener pastures in America. Over 350,000 immigrants settled in the United States. At the age of 20, Tomi, a shipbuilder with the legendary strength of three men, ended up in Minnesota where he called himself Tom Sukanen. There was little need for a shipbuilder in Minnesota, however, so Tom turned to farming. He married a farm girl and fathered four children, three girls and one boy.

Life was difficult for the Sukanen family. In 1911 after 13 years of sweat and toil, Tom, age 33, suddenly decided he had had enough. He left his family, promising to return one day, and headed for Canada in search of his brother, Svante, who had a farm in Saskatchewan. With all his worldly belongings on his back and not a penny in his pocket, Tom walked the entire 1,000 kilometres to his destination near Macrorie, about 150 kilometres northwest of Moose Jaw. He settled about 16 kilometres from his brother and took up farming once more.

Tom kept to himself and worked hard. With amazing technical know-how and resourcefulness, he built several useful machines—a powered grain-thrashing machine, a sewing machine, a camera, a tricycle that didn't require pedalling, and a redesigned car that could be conveniently cranked from the inside. During the lean years of the Depression, Sukanen knit himself a suit out of binder twine. He made and played his own violin. Sukanen even created the pliers which he used to pull his own teeth, as well as a pair of false teeth formed out of bits of steel. He was a huge man, standing about 190 centimetres and weighing 122 kilograms. His neighbours often saw him walking the 10 kilometres to and from town, bent under the massive weight of supplies he carried on his back.

By 1916 Tom had become a successful farmer and received clear title to his homestead. Over the years he managed to set aside an impressive $9,000. Then in 1918, with not a word to his wife and children for seven years, Tom decided it was time to fulfill his promise. He walked back to his old Minnesota farm to reclaim his family.

When Tom arrived at his Minnesota home, he found it abandoned. His wife had died during an influenza epidemic and his children had been scattered to various foster homes in places unknown. His son was the only one Sukanen was able to track down. Father and son tried to walk back to Canada but were stopped by the authorities just 5 kilometres from the border. The boy was instantly returned to his foster parents. Sukanen was threatened with jail and deported. He walked the 1,000 kilometres back to Macrorie, Saskatchewan, alone.

In the spring of 1929 Sukanen disappeared for a month. People recalled hearing him say that he was thinking of returning to his native Finland, but no one knew how he was planning to get there. It was later discovered that Tom had built a heavy rowboat and waited for the spring high waters to make his voyage easier. He paddled along the South Saskatchewan River to Hudson Bay, got a job aboard a freighter and went home to Finland, accompanied by his homemade violin.

Sukanen returned to Canada later that year with a complete set of maps from the Regina Archives. Shortly thereafter, endless shipments of building supplies began to appear on his Saskatchewan farm amid the whispers and gossip of a community devastated by the Great Depression. His friends and neighbours had often heard him say he would build a boat to take him back to Finland but no one took him seriously—until now. Month after month, year after year, Sukanen toiled on his steamship. Standing in front of his homemade furnace, he bent and shaped solid sheets of flat steel into plates for the hull. His ship consumed all his waking hours while his farm lay neglected and infested with weeds. Sukanen's life savings and every drop of energy were poured into the vessel which he built in three separate sections—a keel, a 13.5-metre hull, and a superstructure consisting of a cabin, railings and wheelhouse. He forged his own pulleys, gears and propeller by hand and painted the keel with horse blood to provide resistance to salt water.

For the next six years, through freezing winters and blistering summers, Sukanen drove himself, never stopping to relax or take time off for illness. By the time the ship began to take shape, he was bankrupt, living a hermit's existence in the cabin he crafted, eating the last of his homestead's grain. Strangely enough, Sukanen had a bizarre name for his ship of dreams. He christened it *Sontianen*, which is Finnish for "little dung beetle."

Sukanen had planned to float the three sections of his vessel down the South Saskatchewan River to Hudson Bay where he intended to assemble the parts, then sail the ship across the ocean to Finland—but the river was an agonizing 27 kilometres away. Anchoring a homemade winch by hand and using his last remaining horse, Sukanen began the move in 1937 by dragging the massive keel and hull 6 metres at a time toward the river. Progress was slow and painful. Sukanen was broke but his pride would not allow him to accept help or food from anyone. After two seasons Sukanen had managed to transport his precious "dung beetle" a distance of only 3 kilometres.

The years of hard labour and impoverishment took their toll. Sukanen lost weight and neglected his appearance. His skin was totally blackened from working over the forge, and his hands were rough and bloodied from struggling barehanded with barbed wire. Malnutrition had rotted his teeth, which he extracted, and in their place were ill-fitting steel dentures that caused painful sores and bleeding. The local folk were growing increasingly concerned for Tom's welfare and wary of his odd behaviour. Sukanen's spirits remained strong even as his health waned. When asked why he was building a ship on the prairie, Sukanen responded that he was getting ready for the great flood that was coming. By this time, no one was sure whether he was serious.

Then one day in 1941 Sukanen discovered that the hull, keel and superstructure had been stripped by vandals. All his

The Sontianen, *Tom Sukanen's little "dung beetle." Note the "S" was changed to a "D."*

work, his hopes, his dreams suddenly evaporated and Sukanen was left a broken man. His neighbours notified the RCMP, more to report on his strange activities than to report the vandalism that had occurred. They convinced the authorities to have him committed, using the excuse that his junk was obstructing His Majesty's Thoroughfare. Sukanen was taken to an institution in North Battleford where he deteriorated rapidly and died two years later on April 23, 1943, at the age of 61. He was buried in North Battleford's Hospital Cemetery.

The remains of Tom's ship were towed to a friend's farm where they lay until 1972, when a local farmer named Moon Mullen became interested in the story of Tom Sukanen and the *Sontianen*. Mullen was determined to restore the ship and give it a place of respect in honour of the man who had dedicated his life to it. He convinced the Prairie Pioneer Village and Museum (just south of Moose Jaw) to transport the remains of the ship to the museum grounds. Sukanen's body was exhumed and moved to the museum grounds as well. With the help of provincial funds and personal donations, a small group of volunteers began to restore and assemble the vessel.

The restoration was completed in 1977 but the vessel was misnamed the "Dontianen" instead of "Sontianen." A capital "S" in old style Finnish letters can easily be mistaken for a "D." The error was never corrected. Today the *Dontianen* sits on a slab of concrete, pointing in the direction of Finland. Next to it is a small chapel and a grave containing the body of its builder. After 40 years, Tom Sukanen and his fully assembled ship are together at last.

Henry Hoet's Obsession

THE TINY TOWN OF CARDSTON, ALBERTA, LOCATED ABOUT 80 KILOMETRES SOUTHWEST OF LETHBRIDGE, IS KNOWN FOR ITS COLOURFUL PAST. From the magnificent Mormon Temple in the town's core to its fountain, a tribute to Cardston native Fay Wray (of King Kong fame), many of the landmarks provide a fascinating step back in time.

Henry Hoet (in the middle with arms folded) and co-workers at the Mormon Temple.

Cardston took its name from Charles Ora Card of Utah, who in 1887 began his trek into Canada in search of religious freedom. Leading a party of 41 Mormon pioneers, Card decided to settle northwest of the Milk River, in what is now Cardston. One of the primary tasks facing the young religious settlement was to build a temple for the community. By 1923, after ten years of construction and a price tag of nearly $1 million, the first Mormon Temple in Canada was completed. Perched on a hill, it clearly dominates all other buildings with its sheer size and grandeur.

Another of Cardston's historic buildings has a much more unusual story to tell. Built in 1889, it is known as Cobblestone Manor, one of Southern Alberta's finest restaurants, operated by Arlene and Ed Flickinger since 1977.

Cobblestone Manor was not always a dining establishment. It used to be the home of Henry Hoet. Actually, to call it Henry Hoet's home is a gross understatement for it truly was Hoet's all-encompassing obsession, an obsession that would dominate the best years of his life.

A great deal of mystery surrounds the life of Henry Hoet. Little is known about him. He was described as a recluse and a hermit though his fellow workers always spoke of him as an honest, hard-working gentleman. His only companion was a large, black Newfoundland dog. He led a lonely life of solitude, consumed by his passion and his house. It was said that Hoet was a Belgian immigrant, yet he spoke fluent German. For a time he was employed in a piano factory in New York. Then Hoet came to Cardston to work on the Mormon Temple as a finishing carpenter. The skilled craftsman and artisan had also worked on the construction of the famous Prince of Wales Hotel in Waterton. Many homes in Cardston still have pieces of furniture made by Henry Hoet. Other than his employment history, no one really knew the man at all. He had no family, no friends and no wife, although he had hoped all that would change.

Henry Hoet purchased an old log cabin built by Joseph Young, who came to Cardston from Utah to help establish the

Mormon colony. In 1908 a great flood swept through the town destroying many homes in its path. Although Young's cabin did not suffer too much damage, the property was littered with cobblestones and debris. When Henry Hoet bought the old weather-boarded house, it was assessed at $150. The large lot on which it stood was valued at a paltry $200, but Henry saw beyond the rocks and litter. He knew he had valuable building materials right on his doorstep. Hoet was a man with a mission. Over time he would transform the humble little pioneer cabin into a dream home—one befitting the sweetheart he had left behind in Belgium. Hoet was convinced she would join him as soon as the house was finished. Nothing could keep him from achieving his vision. He became obsessed with getting the house ready for her.

With no one to distract him except his dog, which he harnessed to a two-wheeled cart or a sleigh to help him haul the stones and rocks, Henry spent every spare moment converting his log cabin into a stone house. His only confidant, a nearby neighbour, occasionally helped with some of the heavy labour. Henry covered the exterior walls in cobblestones from his property and nearby Lee's Creek, laying the stones and rocks in mortar and completely changing the appearance of the house. The exterior walls were about 60 centimetres thick. It has been estimated that there are about 180 tonnes of rock in the house, and each rock had been carefully washed before being used.

After finishing the exterior, Hoet began adding rock-walled rooms to the house, one at a time, completely finishing each room before starting the next.

Although he spoke little English, Hoet's skill and artistry in the Mormon Temple brought him special status. As a reward, he was allowed to take home scraps and leftovers of expensive, exotic woods that were imported for the Temple's interior. Henry was often seen filling up his empty lunch pail with little strips of wood, until he collected enough to create his interior masterpieces. He tried to imitate the grandeur of the Temple by piecing together intricate tiles in precision-cut honeycomb patterns for his own interior walls and ceilings. His Golden Oak Room took nearly nine years to complete. The honeycomb design in the ceiling has 61 pieces of oak in each tile. There are a total of 150 tiles covering the ceiling.

Ceiling in the main room of Cobblestone Manor. All the inlaid wood pieces were leftover scraps from the Mormon Temple construction site.

Another room has 125 ceiling patterns, each one with 50 interlocking pieces of wood like a giant jigsaw puzzle. The massive fireplace is covered in small cobblestones coated in a unique mixture of stain and beeswax, giving the stones a shine and ensuring that soot and dirt would never adhere to the surface. Hoet was certain she would have wanted it that way.

As a finishing touch, Hoet imported magnificent stained glass from Europe that he fashioned into Tiffany-style lamps and added to cupboard doors and furniture. In one room, finished in various dark woods, over 40 lights were installed, including indirect lighting behind the cabinetry. This was most unusual in the 1920s when a single light source was often considered a luxury.

Henry Hoet's home was more than an artistic creation. Some of his innovations were state of the art. Each window, for example, was made of two panes of glass held together in a frame. Before putting the panes together, Hoet wiped the interior surfaces with a mixture containing ammonia. Once the panes were sealed, this mixture created an inert gas, providing effective insulation and water resistance. Hoet had created thermopane windows, many of which still exist today.

It took 16 years for Henry Hoet to finish his dream home, but he lived in it for only one year after its completion. It was said that around this time he received a "Dear John" letter from his sweetheart. Henry was heartbroken. Neighbours recalled that he began to act even more strangely than before. He was seen pacing about his property in the middle of the night with his dog, or shooting at woodpeckers who dared to peck at his roof. Children were warned not to go near the house. One resident remembered a time when a cow wandered onto Hoet's property. In a state of confusion, Hoet attacked the cow with his garden hoe, taking a chunk out of the animal's side. Henry's mental state was worsening. Reports of bizarre behaviour were becoming more frequent. In 1927, the town of Cardston had Henry Hoet committed to a mental institution in Ponoka, Alberta, where he died a short while later.

On October 5, 1929, Henry Hoet's fabulous obsession, his cobblestone house, was sold at public auction under the direction of the government. The auction attracted crowds in the hundreds from near and far. The house was described as a landmark, valued anywhere from $20,000 to $25,000 with all its fittings and furnishings. Yet it sold to the Masonic Lodge for an unbelievable $1,200.

The Masonic Lodge owned the Hoet house until 1959. After that, it passed to several different owners until Ed and Arlene Flickinger purchased it in 1977. The house had deteriorated considerably over time. Thus began the painstaking and costly job of restoring the house to its original splendour. Part of the house is used as the Flickingers' residence; the rest has been converted to dining areas. It is with great pride that they named their restaurant Cobblestone Manor.

In June of 1983 the Alberta government recognized Hoet's obsession and designated Cobblestone Manor an historic site. The restaurant is still owned and operated by the Flickinger family. Henry Hoet's sweetheart never came as he had so desperately hoped, but hundreds of visitors have fallen in love with his cobblestone house and the legend of the man who created it.

Henry Hoet's dream house, Cobblestone Manor, is now owned and operated as a restaurant.

Part Two

Schemers

The Last Laugh

CHARLES MILLAR DID TWO TOTALLY UNEXPECTED THINGS ON THE AFTERNOON OF SUNDAY, OCTOBER 31, 1926. The fit, 73-year-old bachelor, who had never missed a day of work, collapsed and died without warning in his office. The second surprise was to leave behind a will so bizarre and outrageous it would surpass everything Millar had ever accomplished during his lifetime.

Charles Millar, prominent corporate lawyer, set out to prove that everyone could be bought, for the right price.

No one could have anticipated that the prominent Toronto lawyer and businessman would create such a media circus, but Millar was determined to prove that anyone can be bought at the right price. In the process, this respectable, proper gentleman set the stage for the greatest post-mortem joke of the century.

Charles Vance Millar began life as a farm boy in the Aylmer district of Ontario. As a student he won top honours, including a gold medal for natural sciences at the University of Toronto. His academic career at Osgoode Hall Law School was equally impressive and he was called to the Bar in 1881. Millar began his career earning a modest wage while living at the Queen's Hotel in Toronto. In time he became a successful corporate lawyer specializing in contract law. With a keen eye for business, Millar bought several homes which became profitable rental properties. He purchased a houseboat with the Chief Justice of the Ontario Supreme Court. For entertainment he raced horses, and owned seven at the time of his death. Two of his racehorses were notable prize winners. Troutlet won the Clarendon Plate, and Tartarean won the King's Plate. Apart from his legal practice, Millar's main business involvement was as president and major stockholder of the O'Keefe Brewing Company.

Those who knew him remembered Charles Millar to be a loving and devoted son. When his father died, Millar left his 23-year residence at the Queen's Hotel to purchase a large home for himself and his widowed mother. He worked long, hard hours at his office, was never known to be sick a day in his life and, whatever the season, always slept in the open air on his veranda.

Millar's funeral was well attended by a distinguished list of mourners from legal, business and sporting circles. The service was conducted by Rev. Dr. T.H. Cotton of St. Aidan's Anglican Church, who spoke highly of the deceased, praising his dedication, morality. and dignity. It would be the last time a clergyman would ever have a good thing to say about the late Charles Millar.

Millar's mischievous will was designed to poke fun at certain "high and mighty" members of society who forced their definition of morality on the public. He stated at the beginning of the eccentric document, "This will is necessarily uncommon and capricious because I have no dependents or near relations, and no duty rests upon me to leave any property at my death."

To his faithful employees he left a small inheritance; to his relatives he left nothing. His reasoning was that if he included them in his will, they would hope for his passing, and Charles Millar did not want anyone to look forward to his death. But, those who did receive a portion of his estate could not have imagined what had possessed the shrewd old prankster to do what he did.

Millar had the most fun with those he considered prim and proper. To every ordained Christian minister in Sandwich, Walkerville and Windsor, Ontario, Millar left one share of stock in the Kenilworth Jockey Club Racetrack. He bequeathed one share of the Catholic-owned O'Keefe Brewing Company to every Orange (Protestant) Lodge in Toronto and to every minister who publicly opposed drinking. The response was overwhelming; most of the recipients came forward to claim their prize.

To a judge and a preacher, both fiery opponents of gambling, he offered lucrative shares in the Ontario Jockey Club, provided they enrolled in the club within three years—which they did, just long enough to cash in their shares and leave.

Three of Millar's lawyer friends who were known to despise one another, inherited his vacation home in Jamaica, which they ended up sharing with great hostility.

As humorous as these dilemmas and their outcomes appeared, they couldn't compare to the most publicized clause of this sensational will. Charles Millar bequeathed the remainder of his fortune to the Toronto woman who produced the most children, under the Vital Statistics Act, during the ten-year period following his death. Naturally, a few distant relatives contested the will, but Millar was one of the top contract lawyers of his day and the carefully written clauses could not be overturned.

Within nine months following Millar's death, the fertility race was on, sparking more controversy than any single item in the news. Mothers who were lucky enough to give birth to twins or triplets made headlines. The press had a field day reporting on the "Great Stork Derby" and posted box scores ranking the women in the lead. The clergy was mortified, claiming that Millar's will promoted immorality by degrading the sanctity of birth. At one point the Attorney-General of Ontario took the case to the Ontario Legislature, trying to revert the $520,000 remaining in Charles Millar's estate to the crown for the benefit of a scholarship fund at the University of Toronto. Local women's groups were outraged, insisting Charles Millar was completely rational when he wrote his last will and testament and no politician was going to cheat deserving women and children out of what was rightfully theirs. Protests were immediately launched. Women's groups were quick to point out that several bequests had already been paid and there had been no complaint when a number of clergymen came forward to collect.

Finally, on the tenth anniversary of Charles Millar's death, the courts were ordered to uphold the terms of the will and decide on the winners. Two women were disqualified from becoming "finalists." One mother had ten children but only five were fathered by her legal husband. Another had nine children, but five were stillborn and the poor woman was unable to produce the necessary birth certificates. Each received a consolation prize of $12,500. The remaining fortune was equally shared by four mothers, each with nine children born during the required ten-year period. Upon receiving over $165,000, each mother had to promise to practise birth control.

The "Great Stork Derby" received more media coverage than Charles Lindbergh's solo flight across the Atlantic or the incredible birth of the Dionne quintuplets. By focusing world attention on the lunacy of uncontrolled breeding, the old bachelor hoped to embarrass the government and the clergy into rethinking their policies on birth control. Charles Millar set out to show just how far people are prepared to go for someone else's money. Perhaps his greatest accomplishment was to prove that he who laughs last, laughs best.

The Great
Groundhog Caper

**CANADIAN FARMERS HAVE LONG RELIED ON THE ACCU-
RACY OF THE *FARMER'S ALMANAC* FOR SEASONAL
FORECASTS.** The rest of the population depends on a more
sophisticated source of information. No, not the scientific
advances of modern technology, but the undisputed predic-
tions of an albino groundhog from Wiarton, Ontario.

*"Willie Emerging," Wiarton's famous rodent is immortalized here in
stone, overlooking Colpoys Bay.*

Akin to his American neighbour, Punxatawney Phil, a Wiarton Willie has emerged from hibernation every February 2 since 1956, amid great pomp and circumstance, to an eager crowd of spectators and the international media who await his annual prediction. Sleepily, Willie looks at the multitudes before him, yawns noticeably and checks for his shadow. If he can see it, there will be six more weeks of winter. If he cannot see his shadow, spring will arrive early.

Willie's handler, Sam Brouwer, holds the famous rodent who "whispers" his prediction into the ear of the town's mayor. The two men, formally attired in their white tuxedos, complete with top hats and tails, turn to face the crowd, relaying Willie's seasonal weather report. Having offered the nation his common rodent sense, Willie yawns once more, and is returned to his burrow.

Wiarton Willie is no ordinary groundhog. He belongs to the marmot family of rodents. His Latin name is *marmota monax*, which means "solitary mountain mouse." Willie was born on the Bruce Peninsula in north central Ontario, precisely on the 45th parallel—the midway point between the North Pole and the Equator. According to the Wiarton Willie Organization, the albino groundhog with the little pink eyes is reported to be correct in his extended weather forecasts about 90% of the time. Environment Canada claims it's all ground-hogwash, but statistics are not nearly as important as the fun and revenue that the festival brings to the region. Approximately 2,000 to 3,000 visitors come to the little town of Wiarton (population 2,200) for the festival, pumping a reported $60,000 to $70,000 annually into the local economy.

The furry white meteorologist has a fan club, a birthday club, a corporate account and an award-winning Web site. Fame and fortune have afforded him a few of life's luxuries, such as the little stone castle that he now calls home. Willie's residence is located on the grounds of the Wiarton Willie Motel. In 1995 Willie was immortalized in stone when the town of Wiarton unveiled sculptor Dave Robinson's *Willie Emerging*.

The world's largest stone sculpture of a groundhog was carved from nearly 7 tonnes of limestone, the same stone that forms part of the Canadian Peacekeeping Monument in Ottawa and the Canadian Embassy in Washington.

The story of the Wiarton Groundhog Festival began in the nearby town of Oliphant over 40 years ago when Mac McKenzie was looking for a way to break up a long and dreary winter. He was working as an aide to the Minister of Health at Queen's Park at the time. As a prank, McKenzie sent out a press release inviting everyone to the world's first International Groundhog Day. The invitation was forwarded to his friends in Ontario, Michigan and Ohio, but the *Toronto Star*, unaware of the joke, sent a reporter to cover the big event. The reporter soon discovered it was nothing more than McKenzie and a few of his friends having a winter bash. Still, he needed a story to take back home, so McKenzie and his party obliged the reporter by sticking one of the guest's large, furry hats into a snowbank and presented Wiarton's first celebrated "groundhog" to the press. The story was published, the hat was later replaced by Willie, and a legend was born.

The job of predicting and reporting the weather, however, is not without its stresses and dangers. As everyone knows, people complain about the weather but no one is able to do much about it. In April of 1996, Willie was placed in protective custody following several death threats. He had predicted an early spring, yet two more bitter months of winter followed and some disgruntled residents grew restless. Sam Brouwer, Willie's handler, admitted that his motel was inundated with angry calls regarding the weather and Willie's incorrect prediction. Then a disturbing, anonymous message made from letters clipped out of magazines arrived at town hall. Staff took the threat seriously and informed the local Ontario Provincial Police. A police spokesperson confirmed that the letter was on file. They kept a watchful eye on the famous rodent until the first signs of spring appeared. Willie had weathered the storm.

Alas, all good things must come to an end. In the winter of

1999, at the age of 22, Wiarton Willie was found dead inside his burrow-castle at the Wiarton Willie Motel. The police later confirmed that foul play was not suspected and that Willie had died of natural causes sometime between November and January. When Sam Brouwer discovered the decomposing remains of Wiarton's famous groundhog, it was just two days before the festival. The festival committee decided to keep Willie's death a secret. The public would not be told the terrible news right away. Hundreds were already celebrating and partying. As with any good entertainment, it was decided that the show must go on. Finally, on Groundhog Day, the announcement was made that Willie had passed away.

Condolences poured in from places near and far—Japan, Australia, Iceland and even the U.S. military. A saddened public filed past their beloved rodent as he lay in his custom-built pine coffin, swathed in pink silk, with two shiny pennies covering his eyes. In his paws he held a large orange carrot. People mourned across the province. Messages came from Ontario premier Mike Harris's office expressing the premier's grief. Photographs of Willie lying in state at the motel that bears his name appeared on the front pages of newspapers across the continent. CNN beamed the image around the world. Willie's Web site received an unbelievable one million hits.

Then suddenly, all hell broke loose. There was an unprecedented media frenzy. Phones rang off the hook. Willie's Web site was bombarded. Finally the Mayor was forced to admit that the groundhog in the coffin was an imposter. It was one of the former Willies who had died years ago and had been stuffed after his demise. Sam Brouwer explained that Willie's rotting corpse was simply "too gross" to be presented to the public. So, knowing that people needed some kind of closure and a chance to say goodbye, the committee substituted a Willie predecessor to preserve Willie's memory with dignity. Willie's unsightly remains were cremated. In July, his ashes were committed to the waters of Colpoys Bay near his statue.

Willie lived a good life, reaching a ripe old age of 22 (about

Preserving a legend. Mourners pay their last respects to the late Wiarton Willie. The mock funeral attracted attention worldwide.

154 in human years). In the wild, groundhogs are not expected to live more than ten years. Survival chances for an albino, with no camouflage from the many predators in the region, are considerably less than the average. Sam Brouwer attributed Willie's longevity to his protected, leisurely lifestyle and his diet of cabbage, cauliflower, carrots and a regular supply of alfalfa. His every medical need was attended to by the local veterinarian who consulted with specialists at the University of Guelph regarding Willie's health issues.

Following Willie's death in 1999, the festival committee decided not to take any more chances. Never again would they find themselves in the awkward position of being groundhogless. Now living in the stone den on the lawn of the Wiarton Willie Motel are two Wee Willies, quickly growing up to assume the same duties as their famous predecessor. The little marmots will take turns sharing the limelight as one or the other predicts the end of winter to an adoring public. They made their debut on February 2, 2000. It was the beginning of a new era.

Sam Kee's Revenge

IT STARTED OFF AS A TYPICAL RAGS-TO-RICHES STORY—LOCAL IMMIGRANT SETTLES IN THE NEW WORLD AND THROUGH PERSISTENCE, HARD WORK AND AN ENTREPRENEURIAL SPIRIT, BECOMES WEALTHY AND POWERFUL. In many ways the Sam Kee story fits the bill, except for an unusual twist or two.

Portrait of Chang Toy as he was often seen, in traditional Chinese attire.

First, the Vancouver landmark that bears his name was built, out of spite. Second, Sam Kee, the person, never existed.

According to *Ripley's Believe It Or Not*, the Sam Kee Building enjoys the distinction of being the narrowest building in the world. Situated on a prominent corner of Vancouver, B.C.'s Chinatown, this mere slice of a building looks more like a long, skinny double-decker tram than a place of business. The building has a 29.25-metre frontage along 8 West Pender Street but is only about 1.5 metres in width. In its day, it housed several businesses, along with living quarters upstairs for an entire family and communal baths in the basement that extended well under the street.

Sam Kee was the name of a firm owned by prominent businessmen Chang Toy and Shum Moon, but company and clients used the name Sam Kee to refer to Chang Toy. By the turn of the century, Sam Kee was one of the most prosperous businesses in British Columbia. As one of the first Chinese firms to actually own land in Vancouver, the company held ten lots in Chinatown as well as five hotels and buildings in central Vancouver and vicinity. Records show that the company paid an annual property tax to the city of over $3,000.

In their day, Chang Toy and Shum Moon ran an extensive import/export trade, operated a rice mill and herring saltery, acted as cash dispatchers between new immigrants in Canada and their contacts back in Canton Province. They even sold steamship tickets for the Blue Funnel Line. With success came prestige and positions of responsibility. Chang became a leader of the Chinese community and a Life Governor of the Vancouver General Hospital.

Chang Toy, the mover and shaker behind the company's success, was born in 1857 to poor peasants in Guangdong Province. In 1874 he moved to Victoria. His boat passage had been paid by a fish canner in exchange for one season of work upon arrival in British Columbia. As luck would have it, the boat arrived late and only one month of work remained. It was just as well. Chang was fired from his cannery job in Victoria after a fight with a racist foreman who had insulted him. Prejudice against Chinese immigrants was widespread in those days but Chang remained proud and defiant. After a few years he moved to Vancouver where he established a variety of different businesses.

Lord Strathcona owned the site of what became known as the Sam Kee Building before it was purchased by the company in 1906. In 1912, the city expropriated 7 metres of Sam Kee's 9-metre property in order to widen Pender Street. The city refused to compensate the firm for the remaining 2 metres of land. Chang Toy, who spoke no English, drove a hard bargain. His attitude infuriated the city fathers, who were only too glad to get even with the successful immigrant merchant dressed in formal silk gown with Mandarin collar. They left the Sam Kee property with what they assumed was a worthless sliver of land about 2 metres wide, along Pender Street. Chang Toy's neighbour was thrilled with the nasty turn of events. He fully expected to buy the valuable corner lot very cheaply, but Chang would not accept defeat. Out of spite, he hired Vancouver's newest architectural firm, Brown and Gillam, to erect a building on what remained of the site. Winning a bet and proving that you can beat City Hall, Chang surprised them all with what became known in 1913 as "Chang Toy's Revenge." The narrow building—that still exists today at the corner of Carrall and Pender Streets—had bay windows all along the second floor to increase the interior space for the upstairs apartment. The living quarters housed a family of five in one tiny bedroom. Small as it was, the apartment came equipped with some "modern" conveniences like a flush toilet.

Chang Toy died in 1920 at the age of 63. Many tenants have come and gone since the building was first erected. Today it is owned and occupied by the Jack Chow Insurance Company. On September 25, 1987, following a major $250,000 renovation, Jack Chow celebrated the "new look" of his building with a splashy opening ceremony. Cutting the red ribbon was the province's premier Bill Vander Zalm, as well as two city aldermen. Fifty-seven years after his death, Chang Toy achieved his ultimate revenge, as these high-ranking public officials paid their respects to a man who stood his ground—and built on it.

The Sam Kee Building. According to Ripley, it is the narrowest building in the world. Businessman Chang Toy refused to give up the choice corner location along Pender Street.

The Lost
Lemon Mine

IN THE SPRING OF 1870, A GROUP OF PROSPECTORS LEFT TOBACCO PLAINS, MONTANA, AND HEADED TOWARD THE HIGH RIVER COUNTRY OF ALBERTA. It was said that gold had been discovered in the hills near the North Saskatchewan River.

Senator Dan Riley, who financed one of the searches for the Lost Lemon Mine.

For most in the party, the trip proved to be a waste of time, but two of the prospectors, Lemon and Blackjack, had come looking for gold, and gold they would find. After a few false leads, they separated from the rest and decided to strike out on their own.

The two turned southward, following an ancient land trail up the High River, stopping along the way to pan for gold in the mountain streams. Sure enough, one of the streams contained the first glittering traces of gold. Lemon and Blackjack began to move upstream, panning excitedly as they made their way toward the source. With every scoop of gravel, more nuggets were uncovered. They knew they were onto something big and began to dig a couple of pits, when they accidentally stumbled upon the rock ledge from which the gold originated. Lemon and Blackjack had discovered the motherlode.

By this time, night had fallen and Lemon and Blackjack, filled with visions of wealth, began to talk business. Before long the two men found themselves in the middle of a heated debate. Blackjack did not share Lemon's patience. He wanted to work the claim immediately. Lemon insisted it was getting too close to winter. He felt they should stake their claim and go back to Tobacco Plains, then return in the spring when the weather was more favourable.

Tempers flared, accusations were made and suspicions grew deeper with the falling of night. The situation was beyond compromise; Lemon and Blackjack realized they would have to divide the claim. But how? Lemon couldn't trust Blackjack to work the diggings alone all winter. There appeared to be no solution.

Exhausted from their adventure, the two decided to sleep on it and settle their dispute in the morning. They wrapped themselves in blankets and bedded down, but Lemon could not sleep. He lay awake thinking, and with every passing minute his imagination grew wilder. Lemon slowly unwrapped his blanket, crept to the pile of equipment scattered on the ground

Father Lacombe (top left), with Jean L'Heureux (the "Pretender Priest") and Stoney Indians (the keepers of the curse).

and picked up an axe. Then, filled with frustration and rage, he struck Blackjack with the axe, splitting his skull.

Lemon soon realized what he had done and panicked. He had to get away before anyone found him. Little did he know that he was not alone. Hidden behind the bushes were two young Stoney Indians, William and Daniel Bendow. They had witnessed everything.

William and Daniel exchanged knowing glances. Gold. If word of the discovery got out, the land they called home would soon be overrun with crazed prospectors. All night long William and Daniel wailed and howled. Their shrieks and groans echoed in the darkness until Lemon was sure he was losing his mind. He wanted desperately to escape but knew he had to wait until dawn.

With the first sign of daybreak, Lemon mounted his horse and fled, leaving the other horses behind. William and Daniel Bendow instantly stripped the campsite and rode back to the Stoney village of Morley where they reported everything to Chief Jacob Bearspaw. The chief shared their fears. He decreed that no one must ever know where the gold was found, and, swearing the two to everlasting secrecy, he placed a curse on the evil site.

In the meantime Lemon rode back to Montana, tormented with guilt and shame. Flashbacks of Blackjack's bloody face haunted him. Sleep was impossible as he recalled the shrieks and howls that filled the night air. Lemon was going insane. With samples of gold rock still bulging in his pockets, he sought out an old friend, a priest with a dubious reputation named Jean L'Heureux. Lemon confessed everything to the "Pretender Priest."

L'Heureux immediately took charge of matters, knowing he could not rely on Lemon in his present state of mind. L'Heureux needed someone stable who knew the lay of the land. He sent an experienced mountaineer named John McDougall to locate the scene of the crime. Within a few days McDougall found Blackjack. He buried the body and built a cairn of stones above the grave to mark the spot. He, too, was unaware that in the shadows of the bushes, watchful eyes had witnessed him burying Blackjack's body. As soon as McDougall was safely out of sight, some of Chief Bearspaw's braves tore down the mound of stones and scattered them all around the site until no trace of the murder or grave remained. The Stoney curse was destined to protect the secret forever.

By springtime Lemon was well enough to travel again. He led a group of prospectors back into the hills to relocate his lost mine. As Lemon approached the old spot he became confused and agitated. None of the familiar landmarks could be found. The other prospectors grew suspicious and began making ugly accusations. In reality Lemon was not that far off the track, but the closer he came to the hidden spot, the more the landscape seemed to change. The others threatened to kill him, which only made matters worse. Raving mad, Lemon was once again forced to return to Tobacco Plains and the protection of Father L'Heureux.

Lemon never fully recovered. Eventually he left the mountain country and his terrible memories behind, spending the rest of his days quietly on his brother's ranch in Texas. The legend and the mine that bears his name became the pursuit of others.

In the meantime, Father L'Heureux organized a party led by John McDougall to return to the spot where Blackjack's body was buried. En route, McDougall decided to stop at a notorious whiskey-post where he ended up drinking himself to death. Father L'Heureux was forced to abandon the search.

Many searchers followed but no one was as persistent as Lafayette French, a rugged mountaineer. French headed into the hills, but before long a mysterious illness stopped him. As soon as he recovered, he set out once more. Armed with a map which he claimed was given to him by Lemon himself, French tried time and again to relocate the mine, but as he approached the cursed site, some powerful force always seemed to push him back.

For the next fifteen years, French repeatedly tried and failed to locate the mine. Finally in the winter of 1883, he sought out William Bendow, one of the Stoney braves who had witnessed the murder of Blackjack. French offered Bendow 25 horses, 25 head of cattle, plus the surrounding pasture if he would lead him to the location where the killing took place. At first Bendow was tempted to accept the offer but, on the second day of their travels, the Stoney brave was suddenly overcome by a terror so powerful that he refused to go on. Bendow abandoned the expedition.

It was several years before Bendow summoned up the courage to consider striking another deal with Lafayette French. In the fall of 1912, French and Bendow set out once more. That night, with no warning or explanation, William Bendow died. The Stoneys were certain that the wrath of the Great Spirit Wahcondah had struck him down for his willingness to betray the secret. They placed his lifeless body on a cart and returned it to the reservation at Morley. On the night of their arrival, Bendow's son-in-law also died suddenly of no apparent cause.

The Stoneys would never again challenge the curse, but Lafayette French was too close to give up his quest. He continued alone for what would be his last attempt to locate the lost mine. After a few days of searching, French thought he had solved the 42-year-old mystery. He could barely wait to share the discovery with his old friend, Senator Dan Riley, who had financed the expedition.

French stopped in at the Bar U Ranch and hastily sent a letter to Riley. He wrote that he had discovered "it" at last, that he was coming up to High River to share the information with the Senator and that he would need help.

French never made it to High River. Late that evening he stopped at an old cabin to get some rest. During the night the cabin mysteriously caught fire. French managed to escape with severe burns. Some men at a neighbouring cabin took him, barely alive, to the hospital at High River. His last request was to speak with Dan Riley. By the time the Senator arrived, French was close to death. With his final breath he told Riley, "I know all about the Lost Lemon Mine now." Dan Riley never did discover what "it" was. Lafayette French lapsed into a coma and never recovered, taking the secret of the Lost Lemon Mine to his grave.

Place marker along the Crowsnest Highway.

The legend, however, did not die with Lafayette French. To everyone's surprise, Chief Jacob Bearspaw's grandson, King Bearspaw, carried on the search for over 70 years, ignoring the tales of the curse surrounding the mystery. He even gave up his rights as a treaty Indian in order to search for the mine and stake his claim as a Canadian citizen. For many years he lived a poor and simple life, never giving up hope that he would find the Lost Lemon Mine. King Bearspaw died in 1979 at the age of 89. Today a simple wooden sign along the highway reads "Lost Lemon Mine Country" and points toward the High River country of Alberta where the legend lives on.

A Pain
Named Butt

JOHN BUTT (OR BUTTS) HOLDS AN UNUSUAL PLACE IN THE CHRONICLES OF BRITISH COLUMBIA. The annoying little man, who decided to make Victoria his home, is the oldest public nuisance on record. He was described as a real character—a lazy, drunken prankster who turned mischief into a fine art. Time and again he found himself in trouble with the law. Before the courts, he could turn on the tears and plead for forgiveness, swearing that this time he had learned his lesson. His name appeared in the local papers more than any other non-public figure, keeping Victorians in stitches as they read about his outrageous antics. He was the biggest pain the city had ever known, but he was a harmless sort of scoundrel and the people of Victoria loved him.

Not much was known about John Butt other than his colourful reputation. He was an Englishman from Australia who arrived in Victoria in 1858 soon after his release from a San Francisco jail. The records show that he had been implicated in a sensational murder and brought to justice by a local vigilante group. While countless thousands headed to the Fraser River Gold Rush on the mainland, Butt decided to seek his fortune in Victoria by taking on a succession of different "careers." He became the city's first (and last) town crier. Butt could be seen standing on busy street corners ringing a loud bell and delivering public messages, advertisements, local news and government proclamations. He was a caricature of a man, described as a fat little fellow wearing baggy, dirty clothes and an oversized belt below his protruding paunch. He would read his announcements in a magnificent tenor voice, but he couldn't resist inserting an occasional ad lib poking fun at prominent citizens or government officials. As if that were not enough, instead of ending his readings with the customary "God save the Queen," he would glance around the block to make sure none of the authorities could hear, before shouting out, "God save John Butt!" Eventually the government learned of his inappropriate outbursts and promptly ended his first career on Canadian soil.

Boozing and brawling were common pastimes for Butt, often resulting in arrests. In highly publicized, entertaining detail, the *Colonist*, a Victoria newspaper, reported how Butt fast-talked his way out of many a conviction. Time and again he was hauled into court for the illegal sale of liquor to Victoria's Aboriginal community. He once told a judge it was unfair that he should be treated so harshly, since the men who sold him the liquor knew perfectly well what he was planning to do with it, making them just as guilty as he was. The judge didn't know how to argue with such a twisted line of reasoning and dismissed the case.

One day Butt decided the time had come to earn an honest living. He passed out business cards to merchants in town offering his services as a street cleaner. With his horse and cart, Butt set out to gather debris from Government Street, loading up his cart with mud and litter. Driving around the corner with the tailgate tipping slightly, he proceeded to deposit the contents all along Yates Street. He then approached the merchants on Yates Street offering to pick up the garbage, which he did, and deposited it once again on Government Street. In this manner, he managed to keep himself gainfully employed for several weeks until the downtown merchants finally caught on to his scheme.

Unemployed once more, Butt resorted to petty thievery and the illegal sale of liquor, which again landed him before the courts. This time he was unable to talk his way out of trouble and found himself facing a jail term. Actually, Butt rather liked it in jail. He was perfectly content to spend his time eating, sleeping and reading, without having to pay for room and board. Unfortunately he was sentenced to three months on the chain gang, and hard physical work was not what Butt had in mind. Suddenly, without warning, he suffered a mysterious, debilitating stroke. Butt was found in his cell, paralyzed from the knees down. The doctors who examined him were not terribly optimistic and offered little hope for Butt's recovery. They promptly transported the repeat offender to the hospital in a handcart.

Emergency room staff attended to him immediately, performing a battery of diagnostic tests. He was poked, pricked and subjected to a variety of painful needles but Butt lay motionless, never moving his lower legs. Convinced that he was paralyzed, the doctors had no choice but to admit him. News of his unfortunate condition was reported in the *Colonist*, and Victorians were saddened that their favourite rascal had met with such a terrible fate.

Butt received special care and attention in the hospital. He lay in a soft, comfortable bed reading religious material, or was carried from his bed to a chair in the sun where he could socialize freely with passersby. Butt played his part extremely well but Dr. James Trimble was suspicious. He had observed Butt from a distance and noted the occasional twitching of Butt's foot when he thought no one was watching. Dr. Trimble ordered Butt to be placed outside, directly under a second storey balcony. Attendants were told to pour ice water on Butt's head from above. After several buckets were emptied, Butt could stand it no longer. He leaped from his chair and dodged behind some bushes. Then, remembering his paralysis, Butt dragged himself along the ground toward the hospital. He was quickly captured and returned to the chain gang where he served the remainder of his sentence.

Upon his release from jail, Butt landed a job at the old Colonial Inn on Government Street. The Colonial had plans to cater an important tea party for a group of church ladies, most of whom were Temperance workers. Butt was put to work in the kitchen when he became "inspired." He emptied two bottles of brandy into the teapots, then waited and watched. The ladies soon become thoroughly intoxicated, much to the delight of Butt who happily observed the scandal he had created.

The next morning the tea party was the talk of the town. Proper citizens of Victoria were outraged, and Mayor DeCourcey was positively livid. Butt overheard the mayor say he would gladly give an entire pound sterling for information on the man who spiked the church ladies' tea party. An entire pound sterling? Butt could not resist. He asked the mayor if he would indeed pay a pound to know the man's name. The mayor willingly agreed, but when Butt admitted that he was the culprit, instead of giving him the reward, the furious mayor grabbed him by the shirt and dealt him several swift kicks to the backside. Butt fled, poor and sore for his troubles.

John Butt's final brush with the law came when he tried unsuccessfully to steal a goose by tucking the huge bird under his coat. When stopped by a constable, he explained that he was taking a bundle of old clothes to a poor woman in the alley. At that very moment the bundle began to honk loudly. John Butt's goose was cooked. He was arrested on the spot and sentenced once again to three months on the chain gang. City officials, however, had had enough. They pardoned Butt after a few weeks on the condition that he leave Victoria permanently. Butt put on quite a performance, weeping and wailing, bidding a tearful farewell to his fellow jail mates and guards.

Along with two other troublemakers, Butt soon signed aboard the *Rodoma*, a ship bound for China. A large crowd gathered at the dock to see him off. With tears and laughter, Butt waved at his fans, then disappeared from view, never to be seen in Victoria again. The *Colonist* which had covered so many of his shenanigans over the years, would print a final goodbye, calling John Butt "the city's gayest rogue."

They Called It
Little Chicago

TODAY IT IS MOOSE JAW'S MAJOR TOURIST ATTRAC-
TION, YET UNTIL RECENTLY CITY OFFICIALS WOULD
NOT EVEN ACKNOWLEDGE THE EXISTENCE OF A
"SECRET" NETWORK OF UNDERGROUND TUNNELS.

*Allen G. Hawkes, Saskatchewan's Liquor
Commissioner during the 1920s.*

During the Roaring '20s, illegal drinking, bootlegging, gambling, prostitution, drug dealing and corruption took place beneath the streets of Moose Jaw, Saskatchewan. Once known as the sin capital of the Prairies, the little town had a reputation that made it one of the most colourful hot spots in all of Canada. They called it Little Chicago.

Legend has it that the most notorious gangster of them all, Al Capone, had dealings in the tunnels. Chicago was Capone's headquarters and much of his illegal liquor was smuggled in from Canada via rail between Moose Jaw and Chicago.

The tunnels have a unique history that dates back to the turn of the century when Chinese immigrant workers faced systematic discrimination in Canada. In 1904, the Canadian government passed the Chinese Immigration Act, introducing a Head Tax. Chinese workers were forced to pay a staggering $500 per person to obtain their immigration papers or risk immediate deportation. Many of them went into hiding, creating a

Walter Johnson, Moose Jaw's Chief of Police, who always kept himself one step ahead of the law.

network of tunnels beneath the city of Moose Jaw as they moved their families and businesses underground.

In 1917, the United States passed the 18th Amendment to the Constitution, better known as Prohibition, which made it illegal to manufacture, possess, sell, export, import or transport any alcoholic beverage. In Canada, Prohibition laws were less strict. Although it was illegal to consume, buy or sell liquor in Canada, alcohol could be manufactured for export. This set the stage for one of the greatest smuggling decades in Canadian-American history as more than one million gallons of Canadian liquor were smuggled across the border every year. Of course, bootleggers had to conduct business away from the watchful eye of Prohibition agents eager to make a name for themselves. In Moose Jaw this was no problem—it all moved underground.

With the arrival of Prohibition, people had to hide their stills, bottles and all evidence of their bootlegging operations. They began to dig in the basements of their homes, hotels and businesses, only to discover they had a captive labour force— countless Chinese people living underground. The Chinese were forced to expand their crawl spaces, enlarge their living areas, and dig an entire maze of tunnels that stretched from the CPR train station, up Main Street, across River Street, and to the many alleyways in between. Bootleggers were soon provided with a direct link to various drinking establishments around town. River Street became the "Red Light" district of the Prairies, while gambling, illegal lotteries and opium dens flourished underground.

Sealed off entranceway to one of the underground tunnels.

It was no secret in Moose Jaw that all this was going on right under the nose of the police department. The odour of alcohol brewing in homemade stills could be smelled blocks away, but the Moose Jaw Police Force turned a blind eye. Not everyone, however, was part of this illegal activity. On opposite sides of the law were two powerful men—Allen G. Hawkes, the tireless Prohibition Agent determined to put an end to the evils of alcohol, and Walter Johnson, Chief of the Moose Jaw Police Department, determined to let it continue.

During Prohibition (1917–1925), Allen G. Hawkes of the Saskatchewan Liquor Commission travelled across the province sniffing out illegal operations. With the persistence of a bloodhound, Hawkes raided hotels, restaurants, recreation centres, bowling alleys, sports arenas, storage sheds—everywhere and anywhere that liquor could be consumed, sold, distilled or hidden.

The British-born Hawkes had come to Saskatchewan in 1886, where he homesteaded until he gained title to a ranch near Swift Current. He was active with the Saskatchewan Grain Growers and the Provincial Breeders Association. Personally, Hawkes was delighted when Prohibition became law. At age 55, the ultra-strict abstainer did not actively seek his appointment to the Saskatchewan Liquor Commission, but was only too happy to accept the position—on one condition. There would be no interference in how he carried out his duties, which he based on the strictest, uncompromising interpretation of the law.

On the other side of the law was Chief Walter Johnson. Johnson came to Moose Jaw in 1905 after nine years on the force in Kenora, Ontario. He was an ardent Liberal, a Mason, an Oddfellow and a member of the Methodist Church alongside Moose Jaw's leading citizens. Johnson spent 22 years as Chief of the Moose Jaw Police Department. Using his political connections for protection, Johnson's personal ambitions often ran unchecked.

Johnson earned less than $2,000 a year, yet was able to purchase a big, new home and a huge model farm after only seven years as Chief of Police. By 1913 his apparent wealth and questionable involvements had raised the suspicions of the Mayor, who hired private detectives to get the goods on the town's Chief of Police. The detectives had no trouble finding evidence of con games, illegal licensing and racketeering that implicated nearly every cop on the force but, on the morning following his re-election, the Mayor ended the investigation and nothing was ever said or done about the report.

In 1922, however, Johnson found himself under investigation again, this time for possession of bootleg liquor. The case ended up in court where Johnson cleverly admitted under oath to "recycling" illegal alcohol that had been confiscated by his department. He claimed that he and his Deputy were simply delivering the contents to leading citizens of the town for medicinal purposes. In a complete turnabout, the investigator (a Liberal) excused the operation, citing the lack of storage space in the crowded little police station. Amazingly, the only one to receive any blame at all was the Mayor (a Conservative) for providing Moose Jaw's finest with such cramped quarters.

The battles between the Mayor and the Chief of Police were nothing compared with the outright war between Johnson and Hawkes. Whenever the Moose Jaw police learned that Hawkes was coming into town to conduct a raid, they would pass a coded message—"There's a storm coming around three o'clock"—to one of the youngsters, who would scurry through the tunnels warning local bootleggers that Hawkes was expected at three o'clock that day. Within seconds the underground tunnel network went into action. Hidden doorways, secret pulleys and concealed passageways were opened to hide all the evidence. The bootleggers could then make their getaway through the tunnels and escape to the other side of town before Hawkes arrived.

Chief Walter Johnson (seated centre) with Moose Jaw's entire Police Force before the big arrest.

There are numerous other accounts of police corruption during this time, but the most famous incident occurred in February of 1924 when more than half the Moose Jaw Police Department was placed under arrest for theft. Shop owners had lodged reports of missing stock over a period of several months but nothing much happened until a parade came to town. Several of the constables' wives attended the outdoor festivities wearing a fashionable assortment of Moose Jaw's finest hats and outerwear. The owner of Robinson MacBean's Department Store recognized his missing merchandise walking about in the crowd. Following an investigation, it was discovered that the constables had been helping themselves to merchandise after hours using the keys that were left at the police station in case of emergency.

The few police constables who remained on the force were released for lack of evidence but they were kept under close surveillance. Chief Walter Johnson was left with nothing more than a skeleton police department.

This unexpected turn of events was just the opportunity Hawkes had been waiting for. In March of 1924, Agent Hawkes raided the Brunswick Hotel. This time there was no one left on the force to send the coded warning through the tunnels. More important, Hawkes had to conduct the raid on his own. Normally he was accompanied by a local police constable who was one of Johnson's boys. The constable would always take Hawkes down to the basement in the hotel elevator so that no one would get caught moving liquor between floors. This time when Hawkes searched the basement, it dawned on him that the elevator was not in its usual place. For years he had raided and searched the hotel, but he had never spotted the trap door that had been at the bottom of the elevator shaft. Sure enough, under the trap door he found a hidden stash of whisky and beer. The owner of the Brunswick Hotel was slapped with a sizeable liquor bill and a stiff fine for breaking the law. Hawkes then made another monumental discovery—the trap door opened up into an underground tunnel that led from the Brunswick Hotel to other establishments along River Street. The gig was up.

Hawkes began searching with a vengeance. It did not matter that Prohibition was about to end; he had a reputation to protect. With the determination of a Sherlock Holmes, the papers said, he conducted a series of lightning raids along River Street. On April 1, 1925, Hawkes and his team of agents ran to the cellar of the Cecil Hotel before anyone was warned. Underneath the main stairway they discovered a trunk filled with 53 bottles of liquor. With great excitement, Hawkes began searching the guest rooms in the basement. Although two of the rooms appeared to be identical, shrewd old Hawkes was suspicious. He proceeded to measure the two rooms and discovered that the second room was slightly shorter than the first. The smaller room was decorated with an unusually oversized calendar hanging on one wall. Hawkes removed the calendar and found the outline of a door leading to a cupboard in the wall. There was the proof he had been looking for. In the cupboard were seven barrels of beer.

On April 15, 1925, Prohibition formally ended in Saskatchewan, but Allen G. Hawkes was not prepared to abandon his fight. He remained with the province's Liquor Commission for an additional ten years, inspecting hotel licences and issuing penalties and fines to anyone who did not follow the letter of the law.

Chief Walter Johnson was asked to leave the force in 1927 after 22 years of service. Johnson stepped down quietly. Eleven years later, in an ironic twist of fate that must have surprised city officials, Walter Johnson was elected Mayor of Moose Jaw, a position he held from 1938 to 1939. He died the following year.

Brother Twelve

HE WAS BORN EDWARD ARTHUR WILSON IN WYOMING, ONTARIO, NEAR SARNIA, IN 1871. His parents—stern, straitlaced and religious—knew their son was a handful but no one could have predicted the fate of little Eddie.

A rare photograph of Edward Arthur Wilson, the notorious Brother Twelve, cult leader and swindler.

Known as Amiel de Valdes, Swami Siva, The Great Guru, The Chela, The God Osiris, The Master, Julian Churton Skottowe and most infamously, Brother XII, many believed Wilson was a mystic, a god or a psychic. In reality, Edward Arthur Wilson was a surprisingly successful con man, proving that a fool and his (or her) money are soon parted.

Edward Wilson had the ability to find a tiny corner of gullibility in each of his followers, many of whom were respectable, intelligent, professional people. He convinced them to abandon spouses, families and bank accounts. Blindly they turned over all their worldly possessions to his evil cult.

Wilson's adventure began at age 14 when irate neighbours pulled up to the Wilson family farm with their pregnant daughter in tow. Young Edward jumped out the window, ran into town, robbed a local store of $70 and never looked back. Searching the globe for answers and staying just one step ahead of the law, Edward Wilson began to dabble in the occult, associating with evangelism, theosophy and black magic. For 12 years he travelled the world visiting exotic shrines and immersing himself in the temples of Egypt, China and Mexico. It was during these travels that Edward Wilson came in contact with questionable religious and occult doctrines from which he formed his own beliefs and philosophies. He took on the role of spiritual diviner, recalling a mysterious past and predicting the future.

In 1924 while in England, Wilson published a book called *The Three Truths*, extolling the virtues of Work, Order and Obedience. He wrote that during a séance he had been transported to the supernatural world where he was presented to a sacred council called the Eleven Masters of Wisdom. These spiritual brothers immediately recognized Edward Wilson as one of the great minds of the living world and made him the twelfth member of the council. Since he was an earthly brother, Wilson was called Brother XII. His task, as outlined by the Eleven Masters, was to establish a refuge for true believers to protect them from coming doom.

People were mesmerized by his teachings and flocked to his side. Among Wilson's first followers were a retired British couple, Alfred and Annie Barley. Brother XII convinced them that his divine mission was to start a new colony on Vancouver Island, a location chosen by the Eleven Masters. He made it perfectly clear that anyone chosen to come to the colony must be totally loyal, silent and unquestioning. Most important, all worldly goods had to be turned over to Brother XII. The Barleys quickly sold their possessions and handed him a total of $14,000 in order to be considered. It was at this time that Wilson met and married a woman named Alma, though rumours abounded that there was another wife whom he had deserted.

In 1927 Wilson officially incorporated his new "organization" under the Societies Act of British Columbia. He called his sect the Aquarian Foundation. Wilson hired Robert England, a former United States Treasury agent with eight years of secret service experience, to be Secretary of the Foundation. England's job at the Treasury Department was to seek out con artists trying to swindle the government. Ironically, he was completely duped by Brother XII.

Robert England was not alone. A scam involving Mrs. Mabel Boyd of North Carolina shows just how far Brother XII was prepared to go to snare a victim. Mrs. Boyd began corresponding with Brother XII after reading some of his literature. She wanted to meet with him before agreeing to join the Aquarian Foundation. Brother XII immediately had her investigated and made some interesting discoveries. He learned that Mrs. Boyd was wealthy and that she had a favourite saint who was able to communicate with animals. That was all Brother XII needed to know.

Two weeks before their rendezvous in a Toronto hotel, Brother XII began intensive animal conditioning. He spent every day on a park bench near the hotel, feeding the pigeons by sprinkling seeds on the ground, on his shoe, on his shoulder and finally, in his ear. After a few days of training, the pigeons flew right onto his shoulder and began picking the seeds out of his ear.

The unwitting Mrs. Boyd arrived in Toronto to meet an eager Brother XII. He told her about his latest revelation of doom, saying he received the message from the Eleven Masters who spoke to him through birds. Mrs. Boyd was suspicious but agreed to accompany Brother XII to his bench in the park. Within seconds the pigeons appeared. One suddenly landed on Brother XII's shoulder and proceeded to place its beak in his ear. Brother XII pretended to have a serious conversation with the bird, convincing Mrs. Boyd that his feathered friend was delivering an urgent message from the Eleven Masters—the end of the world was near and only true believers would be saved. Mrs. Boyd gave him a cheque on the spot for $50,000 and agreed to dispose of all her holdings in order to be accepted into the Foundation. Three weeks later she arrived on Vancouver Island with another cheque in hand. This one was for an astounding $520,000.

One day a fan letter arrived from a wealthy widow named Mary Connally. Enclosed was a cheque for $2,350 with a note suggesting the two meet in Toronto. Brother XII immediately boarded a train in Seattle and headed east. While en route he met the striking Mrs. Myrtle Baumgartner, travelling without her husband. The satanic-looking Brother XII, with his pointed goatee and hypnotic eyes, soon had Baumgartner under his spell. He convinced her that she was the Goddess Isis, destined to save the world by producing the reincarnated Egyptian sun god Horus. Wilson claimed to be the deity Osiris. After a torrid three-day affair, Mrs. Baumgartner agreed to leave her husband and family in order to produce the messiah. Brother XII dropped her off in Chicago while he travelled on to meet Mrs. Connally in Toronto, where he charmed the wealthy widow out of $25,850.

Several days later, Wilson appeared at the Aquarian Foundation with Baumgartner—or Isis—announcing that they planned to live together in his private House of Mystery. His followers, not to mention his wife, opposed this turn of events. Through cleverly concealed microphones, Brother XII learned of the growing discontent on the island. Taking $13,000 of Mrs. Connally's money, he moved with his lover to a newly acquired property, Valdes Island in the Strait of Georgia.

Some followers began to suspect Brother XII was a fraud. Included in this group was the Foundation Treasurer, Robert England, who had Brother XII charged with misappropriation of funds. In a highly publicized lawsuit, Brother XII countered by saying that England had stolen money from the Foundation, an allegation which the former secret agent denied. Things looked bleak for Brother XII until Mrs. Connally swore under oath that she had given the money to Brother XII to use as he pleased. All charges were dropped and Robert England vanished without a trace. In the meantime, Isis never did produce the saviour and, in despair, lost her sanity and was institutionalized.

Of all the followers brought to the Foundation, none was as bizarre or as dangerous, as Mrs. Mabel Skottowe, introduced to the others as Madame Zee, Wilson's second-in-command. Brother XII changed his name to Amiel de Valdes (after his island property) leaving Madame Zee in charge of obedience and discipline, a task she carried out with her famous bullwhip. This cruel, woman derived sadistic pleasure from tormenting the members of the Foundation. She turned her wrath upon poor Mrs. Connally, forcing the 76-year-old woman into slave labour by yoking her to a plow.

Despite it all, the colony continued to grow as more and more believers threw away their life savings in the name of salvation. Brother XII converted most of the currency into 20-dollar gold coins. He put the coins into glass jars, filled the jars with melted wax to prevent the coins from rattling, and placed the jars in custom-made cedar boxes. Over time he accumulated 43 boxes, each containing more than $10,000 in gold coins.

Life at the Aquarian Foundation was spiralling into rituals of evil and torture. Those whose money ran out were forced off the island. Brother XII conducted weekly fertility rites, a privilege in which he alone was permitted to partake. Madame Zee paraded around the compound in silk pyjamas, snapping her bullwhip at anyone who dared oppose her authority.

The two of them must have realized that things were spinning out of control. As members grew bolder and voiced their disillusionment, Brother XII and Madam Zee sensed danger. They loaded all the cedar boxes onto XII's yacht.

Exiled members, now united in their misery and poverty, went to the police. Many had hopes of reclaiming some of their lost wealth. When the police went to the island to investigate, they found the entire colony demolished. Furniture had been hacked to pieces, buildings had been burned, and one of the ships in the harbour had been blown apart with dynamite. Aboard his yacht, Brother XII and Madam Zee disappeared with the gold coins.

After lengthy testimony, the courts awarded a cash settlement to Mrs. Mary Connally, along with title to Valdes Island which had been purchased with her money.

A few years later it was learned that Brother XII had died in Switzerland under the name of Julian Churton Skottowe, Madame Zee's original husband. According to the book, *False Prophet*, however, written by Brother XII's real-life brother, Herbert Wilson, Brother XII died somewhere in Australia. What really became of him, Madame Zee and the gold coins, no one truly knows.

Mary Connally lived out her days among the ruins on the island. One day, while rummaging through the basement, her caretaker came across a sunken vault. He pulled open the latch and found a roll of tarpaper inside. Examining it more closely, he noticed something scratched on the paper. It was the final message from Brother XII to his gullible victims—"For fools and traitors, nothing."

Part Three

Finders, Seekers

From the Amazon
to the Arctic

**DON STARKELL HAS BEEN CALLED MANY THINGS IN HIS
LIFETIME.** He is possibly one of the toughest, most competitive, stubborn examples of human willpower living in Canada today. Starkell's ability to ignore pain and push himself to the outer limits of physical endurance is nothing less than extraordinary.

Don Starkell, age 48, worn and sunburned, off the coast of Venezuela.

He admits that, nearly every year since 1950, he has done something to test his breaking point. At age 33, Starkell swam solo in the icy waters of the Red River for 19 kilometres without any support. Then at age 40, he swam twelve hours non-stop across Lake Winnipeg, a distance of 32 kilometres. Today he prefers to challenge himself by kayaking. He still logs over 1,600 strenuous kilometres per year paddling on the Red River, even though he has lost major portions of his fingers on both hands.

In 1967, Starkell left his job of 16 years as a sales representative at the Canadian Pacific Railway to compete for Manitoba in the Centennial Trans-Canada Canoe Race—a competition that follows the 5,250 kilometre path of the early voyageurs. One hundred and four days later, the Manitoba team was the first of ten canoes to reach the Expo '67 site in Montreal. This was just the beginning for Don Starkell. After the break-up of his marriage in 1970, he spent ten years planning a trip that made history and ended up in the *Guinness Book of World Records.*

On June 1, 1980, 47-year-old Starkell and his two sons, Dana, age 19 and Jeff, 18, set out from their native Winnipeg in a 6.5-metre fibreglass canoe, the *Orellana.* In the end, Don and Dana paddled all the way to the mouth of the Amazon, shattering the world record for distance. Why? To prove to the world and to themselves that they could. In total they travelled over 19,000 kilometres, taking an estimated 20 million paddle strokes along river and stream and into the pounding waves of the open sea. The ocean portion of their trip (a distance of 9,600 kilometres) was longer than any of Columbus's four voyages of discovery. The Starkells' itinerary took them from Winnipeg, along the Red River, down the Mississippi River to New Orleans, along the coasts of Mexico and Central America, and on to Venezuela and Trinidad. From there they entered the mouth of the Orinoco River, into the Rio Negro, and finally along a 1,600 kilometre portion of the Amazon River to where it empties into the Atlantic Ocean at Belém, Brazil. Along the

Don Starkell (left), Jeff (middle), and Dana (right), shortly after launching the Orellana.

way the Starkells came across all manner of life, from whales and piranhas to crocodiles and anacondas, but the most dangerous animal of all proved to be the human kind. Some were charming, generous and hospitable. Others were suspicious, hostile, and deadly.

Perhaps if Don Starkell's childhood had not been so painfully difficult, he would not have been as motivated to do what he did as an adult. Growing up in a Winnipeg Children's Home from the age of two, and then two foster homes, young Don felt controlled and insignificant. He was just one of many children yearning for a better life. After his divorce, he wanted more than ever to feel like a somebody—to make his mark. In the process, he also hoped to provide a challenge and an education for himself and his sons. It would be the experience of a lifetime for all of them.

Starkell had many concerns regarding the voyage. His son Dana had been severely asthmatic for 12 years and was heavily dependent on medication. Dana's physician advised against taking such a life-threatening trip. Don, on the other hand, believed that the medication was contributing to his son's condition and hoped that exercise, fresh air and freedom from all the drugs and allergy shots would improve Dana's condition. Another problem was his son Jeff. Although interested in the venture, Jeff was a serious electronics student who worried about a two-year interruption of his studies and social life. Jeff's presence was necessary for several reasons. His moral support, strength and athletic skill were greatly needed in paddling the vast distance. He also had an uncanny ability to fix almost anything.

Dana also had taken time out from his social life, rock bands and studies in classical music. Among the supplies aboard the *Orellana* were books on electronics for Jeff and music books for Dana. Riding on top of the load was Dana's classical guitar in a waterproof vinyl case.

After months on the Mississippi, the threesome reached the Gulf of Mexico just in time for hurricane season. Discouraged by the high ocean waves constantly overturning their canoe, they were forced to stop. Stuck in Vera Cruz for four months, Jeff grew restless and returned home to complete his education. Don and Dana continued the trip without him.

If Dana and Don had known just how many times their lives would be threatened during the remainder of the trip, they might have decided to go home as well. To make up for lost time, father and son tried to paddle non-stop from Belize to Honduras. They had been warned about the dangers in Guatemala, Nicaragua and Colombia. Nobody had mentioned possible problems in Honduras, where they were accused of being Nicaraguan spies on one occasion and Sandanistan agents on another. At one point Don and Dana were forced to their knees, execution-style, after being robbed at gunpoint. Miraculously their lives were spared.

Don and Dana managed to paddle away from the Honduran border straight into the war zone of Nicaragua, where they were "sea-jacked" and then greeted on a pier by a soldier with a machine gun. This time Don and Dana were arrested and accused of being American CIA spies. Their canoe was thoroughly searched and all camera equipment, film and maps were confiscated. The following morning their maps and camera (minus the film) were returned along with a warning to get out of Nicaragua immediately. They had just passed the one-year mark of their voyage.

In Colombia the determined duo was robbed several times, beaten with bamboo poles and threatened by drug-dealing pirates. Thankfully a Cartagena family proved to be much more hospitable. They invited the hungry travellers to a sumptuous feast featuring a variety of unfamiliar specialties of the house. The Starkells finished their unusual meal with a bowl of crunchy brown *hormigas* for dessert. The tasty little morsels were slightly salty and highly nutritious. After having their fill, they learned that *hormigas* were ants.

By January 4, 1982, Don and Dana had left the open sea and entered the mouth of the Orinoco River in Venezuela. The Orinoco is a waterway filled with toothy pirhanas, deadly stingrays and electric eels so powerful they can knock over a horse. The strenuous trip upstream was generally without major incident, other than a close encounter with a huge anaconda, from which they managed to escape.

On March 12, 1982, Don and Dana reached Brazil, the thirteenth and final country on their voyage, but the Brazilian Military Base at Cucui would not grant them entry into the country. Fortunately the Starkells had in their possession a letter from the Brazilian Ambassador to Trinidad whom they had met en route. The Ambassador had been quite impressed with the Canadian travellers and provided them with a letter of support for their venture. The local Brazilian officials reluctantly allowed Don and Dana access to the Rio Negro and the Amazon River. On May 1, 1982, nearly two years after

Don Starkell, age 57, just before the launch of his first Arctic trek.

leaving Winnipeg, a victorious father and son arrived in Belem, Brazil. Ten days later they hoisted their canoe and remaining equipment onto a cargo ship and headed home to a family reunion with Jeff.

In 1987 Starkell published a bestseller entitled *Paddle to the Amazon*, based on his journal (an estimated one million words) which he had faithfully kept throughout the two-year voyage.

No sooner had Starkell completed this incredible goal, than he was already thinking about new challenges. Later he would point his kayak north and attempt to conquer 5,000 kilometres of icy Arctic waters in a single summer. This trip would take him from Churchill, Manitoba, along the shores of Hudson Bay, across the Northwest Passage to Tuktoyaktuk, Northwest Territories. He started this trek on June 15, 1990, alone, at the age of 57, but the voyage was soon plagued with one

Don Starkell , age 58, on northwest Hudson Bay.

disaster after another. On his third day out to sea Don struck a hidden boulder and capsized in a thawing ice field. Unconscious for an hour, Starkell barely survived the ordeal. After a week on land he began his retreat back to Churchill, but soon discovered that his kayak was leaking. By the time he reached Churchill, Starkell was in a state of shock. The trip was over—for the time being.

The following year Starkell tried again, this time with two partners, Fred Reffler and Victoria Jason. On the second day out of Churchill, the three travellers were icebound, stuck amid freezing cold temperatures, bitter winds and high waves. Being trapped for 16 days on shore, not to mention being stalked by a polar bear, was too much for Fred Reffler. After 22 days, Fred was forced to quit with an arm injury. Victoria was persuaded to go on and after 62 days, Dan and Victoria arrived at Repulse Bay, right on the Arctic Circle. With over 3,000 kilometres to go, and a bay ahead still filled with ice floes, they were forced to return to Winnipeg, and resume the trip a year later.

On June 3, 1992, Don Starkell, age 59, and Victoria Jason, age 47, attempted to pull their loaded kayaks on sleds over ice and snow for 600 kilometres from Repulse Bay to Spence Bay. Timing was critical. They had to reach Tuktoyaktuk by September 15 before the sea turned to ice. In a kayak, having the water freeze up on them would mean certain death. To make matters worse, Starkell refused to carry a 2-way radio or spare paddle for fear it would make him dependent, careless and overconfident. The only technology he would allow was a GPS (Global Positioning System) that used satellite tracking to give precise latitude and longitude readings. After several gruelling days of hauling the loaded-down kayaks 25 kilometres a day, they arrived in Gjoa Haven on King William Island —the place where the Franklin expedition had met its fate when Sir John Franklin's two ships and crew of 129 men died in 1848. It was here that Vicki collapsed from severe exhaustion and was forced to quit the trip. Don continued alone.

Twenty kilometres from the mainland, the ice turned to mush, making it impossible for Starkell to paddle his kayak. Instead he had to pull it back to shore by hand, zigzagging to find solid ice. For nine hours Starkell struggled in freezing winds, often falling through the ice and suffering the effects of hypothermia. Amazingly Starkell managed to get within 50 kilometres of Tuktoyaktuk, but the weather was rapidly closing in on him. Starkell was left stranded in a collapsed snow-covered tent on a sandbar in a freezing sea. He was so low on food he didn't eat for five days, surviving on a single cup of water. Even worse, his kayak was white, making detection by air next to impossible in the swirling snows.

On the sixth day, Starkell heard the familiar roar of an airplane. It circled around, flew low and after three passes, appeared to spot him. Then it left. Two hours later a rescue helicopter arrived and plucked the half-dead, hallucinating Starkell from the frigid Arctic tundra. It turned out that Dana (in Winnipeg) was frantic when he did not receive a pre-planned call about his father's safe arrival in Tuk. After nine days Dana feared the worst and called for a search.

Don Starkell recuperated from his terrifying ordeal but not without a permanent reminder of his brush with death in the Arctic. Frostbite led to gangrene in his fingers, palms and toes, turning them black and useless. He waited an unbelievable two and a half months after returning to Winnipeg before seeking medical attention. All of his fingers and four of his toes had to be partially amputated. For the first year following his surgery, Starkell admits he experienced such pain and sensitivity in his hands he couldn't even push the buttons on his telephone. He stopped experiencing shooting pains in his feet after five excruciating years, yet he has no regrets. Starkell published his remarkable northern adventure in a second book, *Paddle to the Arctic*, in 1995.

At age 67, Don Starkell enjoys his memories but still looks for new challenges. In 52 years of paddling he has logged over 80,000 kilometres—the equivalent of two trips around the world. His son Jeff is a successful electrical engineer living in the Toronto area. Dana, who recorded his third classical guitar CD in Iowa, has not taken any asthma medication since leaving on his canoe trip to the Amazon. As for their amazing father, Don can be found in his kayak perfecting a new method of paddling using only the palms of his hands and his little stubbled fingers. His stroke is strong and rhythmic. He laughs with pride that he does not wear a life jacket and, even with his partial fingers, can still out-paddle almost anyone on the Red River.

The Mushrow
Astrolabes

**WAYNE MUSHROW WAS ALWAYS VERY PROUD OF HIS
HOMETOWN, PORT AUX BASQUES, NEWFOUNDLAND, BUT
ONE THING BOTHERED HIM.** When tourists got off the ferry
at Port aux Basques, Mushrow complained, they either headed
east to the capital city of St. John's, or north to visit Gros
Morne National Park or the Viking Settlement at L'Anse aux
Meadows. Port aux Basques was merely a stopover.

*The Mushrow Astrolabe. This solid brass instrument measures 197
millimetres in diameter and weighs a little more than 4.3 kilograms.
The markings O/Y DYAS are the same as those on an astrolabe
recovered from a 1641 Spanish shipwreck in the Caribbean.*

Wayne Mushrow hoped to change that by giving the government a priceless gift. All he ever wanted was to bring an element of pride and prestige to his hometown and encourage tourists to stay awhile and visit. And he wanted someone to say "thank-you." He never intended to go to battle with his own government.

It began on November 26, 1981, when Wayne Mushrow, a milkman by trade, went scuba diving at Isle aux Morts with his brother, Lloyd, and a friend, Walter Bennett. Mushrow's interest in scuba diving began as a hobby, but occasionally he offered his services to the RCMP, searching for bodies off the southwest coast of Newfoundland. Mushrow had heard about an old shipwreck near Isle aux Morts, about 12 kilometres east of Port aux Basques. The *Despatch*, an Irish vessel, had sunk there in 1828. Mushrow and his companions went down to see if there was anything left to salvage from the wreck after so many years. Wayne never expected to come across the remains of another, much older, shipwreck.

The men found buried in the sand a large anchor, two cannons, some wooden bowls, a green vase, several dishes and five French coins dated 1638. Then, swimming near the sandy bottom, Wayne noticed something shiny, no bigger than the head of a match, sticking up from the sand. It was the tip of an instrument buried for centuries and polished by the shifting sands. Wayne carefully unearthed the strange round object and put it in his catch bag, unaware of what he had found. It was thoroughly tarnished and encrusted with a blackish scale. Mushrow took it home and scrubbed it clean with oven cleaner and steel wool (museum curators would later cringe at the thought). When it was cleaned up, the shiny brass object appeared to be in mint condition. Mushrow saw the date 1628 clearly etched on one side, as well as the letters O/Y DYAS. There were degree markings around the top half of the circle. It looked like an early compass of some kind. Mushrow checked his home encyclopedia and learned that it was an astrolabe, an ancient navigational instrument used by the early explorers to

The World's Largest Astrolabe. Wayne Mushrow and Mayor Sheaves of Port-aux-Basques next to the large scale model of Mushrow Astrolabe I, located just outside the Gulf Museum.

determine latitude by measuring the angle of the sun. Excited by his discovery, Mushrow bought a book on astrolabes. He learned that the artifact he had recovered was a rare collector's item, and knew then that his discovery was worth a fortune.

Mushrow had some photographs taken of his astrolabe and mailed them to different museums in Canada, the United States and Britain. This innocent correspondence marked the beginning of Mushrow's troubles with the Newfoundland government, who suspected that the diver had plans to sell the astrolabe to the highest bidder. They were not about to take a chance on having Canada lose yet another priceless astrolabe, considering what had happened to the last one.

In 1867 an astrolabe had been discovered in Cobden, Ontario, by fourteen-year-old Edward Lee who offered to sell it to a Captain Cowley for ten dollars. Lee didn't get his money or see the astrolabe again. The shrewd captain had realized its value and sold it. After passing through several different owners, the astrolabe was eventually willed to the New York State Historical Society, where it remained until June, 1989. It was then acquired by the Canadian Museum of Civilization in Hull, Quebec. The federal government purchased this astrolabe from the New York Historical Society for a reported sum of $250,000 (U.S.). The astrolabe, dated 1603, is attributed to Samuel de Champlain, the famous explorer. When Wayne Mushrow found his astrolabe, the Champlain astrolabe was still the property of the New York State Historical Society. The Newfoundland government was understandably paranoid about Canada losing another one.

According to Mushrow, he contacted the RCMP to inform them of his find. They did not seem terribly concerned about it. Mushrow appeared on national television to talk about the historical importance of his discovery. During the telecast, Mushrow stated that he wanted to have the astrolabe named after him and made the centrepiece of the museum in Port aux Basques. As for payment, he only requested compensation for his expenses. His real interest was to promote tourism in his hometown. Again, no one seemed terribly interested.

A few months later, Mushrow made another television appearance where he caught the public's attention by mentioning that the astrolabe was probably worth well over $100,000. This time the Newfoundland government was quick to respond, informing Mushrow of the Historic Resources Act which states that all archeological artifacts found on land or in Newfoundland waters are the property of the Crown. Government officials promised Mushrow that the rare find would indeed be placed in the new museum at Port aux Basques. The issue of compensation was yet to be decided. No mention was made of having the astrolabe named after Wayne Mushrow, as he had requested.

After being told what a fine upstanding citizen he was, Mushrow invited the government officials to his home to see the astrolabe for themselves. A small party of men appeared at his door. They were introduced as the Deputy Minister, the Curator of the museum in St. John's, an underwater archeologist, and another gentleman, a Mr. McGuinness, who was not identified by title. The guests were all provided with lunch, at which time Mrs. Mushrow recognized McGuinness as an undercover RCMP constable from a previous visit to a neighbour.

Wayne Mushrow was furious at the sneakiness of the visit. It was then that the Deputy Minister told him that he had come to the house with a letter from the Justice Department. Mushrow was being investigated for diving for artifacts without a permit, for possessing artifacts without reporting them to the Newfoundland government, and for extortion.

Mushrow was speechless. Extortion?! He was told in no uncertain terms that since he had property belonging to the Crown which he would not turn over to the authorities unless his conditions were met, he was guilty of extortion. Mushrow was then told he could face up to 14 years in prison for his "crime." In addition, the Historic Resources Act states that a fine of $50,000 and a jail term of one year can be imposed for every day that an artifact is withheld. Mushrow was dumfounded. He had invited the men to his home as a gesture of goodwill.

RCMP Constable McGuinness made a telephone call, and a short while later a police constable appeared at the Mushrow home with a search warrant for the artifact. The astrolabe was not hidden at the time. In fact it was hanging from a nail on an overhead beam in Mushrow's basement. The police never did find it. They searched until 2:00 a.m. and no one ever thought to look up. While they tried to talk the cool, calm diver into handing over the astrolabe, it had been hanging over their heads the whole time. The frustrated officials went back to St. John's empty-handed.

Some time later, Mushrow and the Newfoundland government came to a verbal agreement. Mushrow was promised that if he turned the astrolabe over, his conditions would be met and he would receive some small compensation for his efforts.

Mushrow, along with the president of the Southwest Coast Historical Society, handed the astrolabe over to the RCMP in February, 1982. Mushrow claims that he never received so much as a thank-you from the Newfoundland government. No mention was made of having the astrolabe named after its finder. To add insult to injury, the Newfoundland Museum in St. John's kept the astrolabe in their basement, only putting it on display in the Gulf Museum in Port aux Basques for about eight weeks every summer. Mushrow's fear was that at any time, the St. John's museum might find a reason to change its mind about having the astrolabe on display in his hometown.

After many years of transporting the artifact back and forth, Mushrow came to realize that he had lost all control over it. But he had a valuable trump card that he was now ready to play. Mushrow insisted on an agreement in writing from the government before he would hand over another astrolabe in his possession. He had discovered the second astrolabe in the summer of 1983 while scuba diving with a friend. It appeared to be even older than his first find.

Mushrow was highly secretive about the second astrolabe and would not divulge any details about it, such as where it was found, the date on it, or where it was hidden. In fact it was dated 1617 and inscribed with the name Adrian Holland, most likely its maker. Mushrow wrote the government a series of letters stating that he would turn over the second astrolabe on November 26, 1991 (on the tenth anniversary of the first astrolabe finding) if, and only if, he received a commitment in writing that both astrolabes would be named after him and kept on display in the Gulf Museum. Mushrow had some lawyers write up an agreement assuring custodial management of both astrolabes in Port aux Basques. For a long time the government refused to sign the agreement, saying that they could not sign for something they had not seen. Mushrow's reply was that they would never see it until they signed for it, and so the second astrolabe remained a mystery. At the time of this impasse, Mushrow was still facing possible criminal charges, and his legal expenses continued to grow.

Twelve frustrating years later, Mushrow received some of the recognition he deserved. In 1993 the first astrolabe was officially named the "Mushrow Astrolabe," and a plaque containing all the information relating to it would accompany the artifact wherever it was displayed.

Mushrow remained disillusioned and disappointed, however, with the treatment he had received from the province. He claimed it a sad state of affairs when an honest person is prepared to give the government a gift which might contribute to local history and community pride and, in return, is treated like a common criminal.

After lengthy negotiations, a written agreement was reached between Wayne Mushrow and the Government of Newfoundland and Labrador, the Southwest Historical Society, and the Town of Channel-Port aux Basques. On February 9, 2001, the second astrolabe was given to the town. The agreement stated that the priceless artifacts would be named "Mushrow Astrolabe I" and "Mushrow Astrolabe II." They would be exhibited in Port aux Basques from June 1 to September 30 every year. The exhibit would include the story of Mushrow's discovery of the artifacts. Finally, no criminal charges would be filed against Mushrow.

Mushrow did not ask for any financial compensation to cover the years of legal expenses, even though it took over 19 years to receive the recognition and the thanks he had been waiting for. He said the astrolabes were his personal gift to his hometown. The agreement stated: "... the Government of Newfoundland and Labrador wishes to recognize the public service which Mr. Mushrow has performed for the people of the province by his discovery of these two astrolabes." For Wayne Mushrow, that was payment enough.

Wild Bill Peyto

HIS NAME IS SYNONYMOUS WITH BANFF BUT HIS LEGEND EXTENDS THROUGHOUT THE CANADIAN ROCKIES WHERE FAMOUS LANDMARKS BEAR HIS NAME—PEYTO LAKE, PEYTO PEAK AND PEYTO GLACIER.

Bill Peyto, all dressed up, hoping to entice a mail-order bride.

On the commercial side, tourists can find Wild Bill's, Banff's Legendary Saloon. His portrait, with its piercing eyes and untamed look, dominates the welcome sign to town. He was the ultimate mountain guide—rugged, skilled and daring, forging paths across sheer slopes of rock. He was Wild Bill Peyto.

Peyto's appearance set him apart from the rest. Those who knew him lived in awe of him. He wore a small sombrero tilted to the side, a kerchief around his neck and a fringed buckskin coat. He dressed the part of a cowboy, all rough and tattered. His frayed, faded pants were torn to the knee, revealing the second pair he wore underneath. Peyto's behaviour was often as wild as his appearance. It was said he used to silence alarm clocks with a pistol, but it was his bizarre escapades and mischievous sense of humour that made him a legend.

One night Bill Peyto casually strolled into a bar with a live lynx strapped to his back. The animal was sedated, but not for long. Without so much as a word, Peyto untied the wildcat, then sat back to enjoy the chaos that followed, as drunken

A visitor's first introduction to Banff.

Peyto Lake, high in the Rockies, is a part of Bill's legacy. It is also known for its unique colour and shape: Note the profile of the dog.

patrons stumbled over one another scrambling for the exit. The lynx escaped untouched and later became a star attraction at the Banff Zoo. Peyto became a star attraction at the local bar.

Another incident illustrated Peyto's peculiar sense of frontier justice. When he and an acquaintance approached the front door of his cabin, Peyto began throwing stones through the doorway until he heard the familiar snap of a bear trap from within. He explained to his companion that he suspected a trapper was stealing food from his cabin. The companion was horrified at the idea that the intruder would have been killed in the trap, but Peyto simply replied that at least he would have known for sure that the man was the thief.

When it came to his pack animals, however, Peyto showed true kindness and compassion. As a guide, he never over-worked his horses, often to the frustration of his party who were eager to push on. During difficult expeditions, Peyto's first concern was for the welfare of his horses. He would lead them to a stream, wash them with care and smear any raw spots with bacon grease to keep away irritating flies.

Ebenezer William Peyto (pronounced Pee-toe) was born in Kent County, England, in 1869. At age eighteen he immigrated to Canada and headed west on the brand new Canadian Pacific Railway. The first important contact in his new home was pioneer guide Tom Wilson, the discoverer of Lake Louise. By 1895 Bill Peyto had proven his worth and became chief guide for Tom Wilson's tourism business in the early days of Banff National Park.

Peyto was the first person to reach the summit of Mt. Assiniboine, nicknamed "the Matterhorn of the Rockies," a feat that everyone thought was impossible. The heroic mountain man was also credited with rescuing Mrs. Winthrop Stone as she clung to a ledge high upon Mt. Eon for eight days after her husband had fallen to his death.

In 1900 Peyto volunteered for the Boer War, serving with Lord Strathcona's regiment of Western Canadian Cavalrymen. Actually, he and a friend flipped a coin to see who would enlist and who would stay home to look after their interests in a small copper mine near Banff. Peyto lost. En route to South Africa, Peyto visited his parents in England. His mother had prepared a comfortable room and a feather bed for her son's arrival but found him sleeping on the bare floor instead.

During the Boer War, Peyto's colourful reputation and bravado earned him his corporal stripes. Stories were told of how he used to gallop on horseback in front of enemy lines to draw their fire, thus revealing their location. He carried an old umbrella with him on these missions. If he suspected an ambush, he would dismount and parade back and forth with his umbrella opened high in the air to draw enemy fire, a practice he continued for six months. Two horses were shot out from under him but Peyto escaped unharmed. Unfortunately the promotion was short-lived. Peyto lost his corporal stripes and two months' salary for one of his pranks. He "borrowed" an officer's coat with several bottles of liquor in the pockets. When the officer demanded the coat be returned, Peyto was forced to comply, but the coat was considerably lighter by then.

Peyto returned home in 1902 to his old life and a new wife, Emily Wood, the sister of a fellow guide. For a while Bill and Emily found happiness. They had a son, Robin, but four years later tragedy struck. Emily died suddenly, leaving the young boy in the care of his bewildered father. Peyto sent Robin to live with his mother's cousin in British Columbia and the mountain man returned to the back woods to find solace.

In 1911 Peyto became warden of Rocky Mountain Park, fighting fires, catching poachers and building cabins in the wilderness. In 1913 he joined the warden service of Banff National Park. With the outbreak of the First World War, Peyto was once again called to duty. He served with the 12th Mounted and Machine Gun Brigade until he received a shrapnel wound to the right leg in the Battle of Ypres, France. For 24 hours Peyto lay in pain, allowing a wounded comrade to leave for medical attention before him. He dressed his wound himself until help arrived. During his evacuation, Peyto stopped along the way to amputate the leg of another soldier, with a knife.

Peyto returned to a hero's welcome in Banff but, in his typically shy and unpredictable way, he hopped off the train before it arrived in town in order to avoid the crowd waiting to greet him.

In the summer of 1921 Peyto married Ethel Wells, the sister of a Banff photographer. Like Peyto, she had emigrated from Britain and, more important, was prepared to tolerate his long absences and strange behaviour, which was becoming increasingly more eccentric.

Peyto became reclusive and paranoid, building cabins in remote hiding places and giving them unconventional names. Where most Banff thresholds bore welcome signs that read "Tumble In," Peyto's signs said, "Tumble Out." His cabin in Banff was named "Ain't It Hell," an indication of the hardships he encountered. There are stories that he built some of his cabins underground and that some were built with mountain streams running right through them. One in particular revealed his unique construction style. Most cabins of the period were built with logs laid horizontally. Peyto, however, used free-standing trees set within vertical log walls. The half-decayed remains of Peyto's 50 or so cabins were discovered years later dotting the entire mountain country in the most unexpected, hidden locations.

Ethel's death in 1940 ushered in a new time of sadness for Peyto, but he remained active, concentrating on his large fossil collection. He even tried to enlist for active duty during World War II at the age of 71. Sometime in the winter of 1942, Peyto learned he had cancer and secluded himself in one of his cabins, refusing to see anyone. He died in March, 1943, in the Colonel Belcher Hospital in Calgary, and was buried in the Banff Cemetery. With his passing, a great era of adventure and exploration in the Canadian West ended.

Tilikum Voyage

NORMAN KENNY LUXTON WORE MANY HATS DURING HIS LIFETIME. His unusual claims to fame ranged from South Seas poker player to honorary First Nations chief back home. Luxton was born on November 2, 1876, in Winnipeg, where his influential father was a founder and editor of the *Winnipeg Free Press*.

Norman Luxton in Banff, holding a model of the Tilikum.

Like his father, Luxton was a journalist, working for the *Calgary Herald*, but he soon became restless. After a brief stint prospecting for gold in the Cariboo, Luxton and a partner began publishing a local gossip-style tabloid in Vancouver called *Town Topics*. When that failed, the young journalist decided to try something totally new. He did not want to write about other people's adventures; he wanted one of his own.

In 1901, 20-year-old Norman Luxton met a Danish-born sea captain over a beer in a Vancouver bar and proposed an idea. It was monumental, it was dangerous, it was downright crazy, but the captain loved it. Norman Luxton and Captain John Voss, an old eccentric with a mysterious past, formed a partnership. Together they would embark on a wild adventure —an ocean voyage around the world. Their vessel of choice turned out to be a 100-year-old native Siwash dugout, 9 metres in length, carved from a single red cedar log. Luxton bought it for eight dollars.

The Tilikum, *fully restored, is on permanent display at the Maritime Museum in Victoria.*

With the help of a carpenter, the ancient war canoe was fitted with a small cabin and watertight storage areas, 3 masts and 4 sails. The unusual bowsprit head was carved by Luxton himself. As for navigational equipment, the odd duo relied on one small sextant with a cracked mirror, a small pocket compass, a watch and an 1884 South Pacific directory and ocean chart. For protection they had one rifle, one shotgun, one pistol and an ancient, small-bore Spanish cannon, which proved more valuable than either of them could have imagined. They christened the converted dugout *Tilikum*, a Chinook word meaning "friend."

On May 20, 1901, Luxton and Voss left Victoria, British Columbia, in search of excitement and discovery. Unfortunately neither the boat nor the partnership lived up to their expectations. The two men had several heated differences of opinion on their journey. On one occasion Luxton grew so frustrated with Voss, he locked him in the cabin and tied the tiller. And in the Doldrums, a region of dead calm around the equator, the temperatures climbed so high they could not step barefoot onto the scorching deck. After 17 days of being stuck in these waters, their food supply had gone bad and their water tank was empty. The relationship between Luxton and Voss was more than a little strained and the two men sat at opposite ends of the canoe with firearms ready, but they refused to return home.

Luxton and Voss managed to overcome a variety of hardships during the dramatic voyage to 42 different South Sea islands. While in Samoa, Luxton found himself short of money and replenished the *Tilikum*'s cash box by teaching the locals to play poker. His most eager student was the Samoan governor. Fortunately the *Tilikum* set sail before the governor was good enough at the game to win back his losses.

At another small island, the chief was so impressed with young Luxton that he offered him one of his daughters in addition to a substantial coconut grove. Luxton knew that he would have to reject the royal offer with great care or else be fed to the sharks. After three days of delicate diplomacy, Luxton was able to talk his way out of becoming the royal son-in-law by promising to return to the island after his voyage. The chief agreed to the delay but held a huge feast—and wedding—for the young couple anyway.

Luxton and Voss set sail again, this time stopping for food and water at the tiny island of Ninafou where Luxton was captured by cannibals and taken to their leader. The chief examined the edible "long pig" while the cannibals sat eagerly staring at their dinner. Luxton had no intention of ending his voyage in a stew pot. He challenged the chief to a contest of speed. The short, wiry Luxton managed to outrun the natives to the safety of the *Tilikum*. Once on board, Luxton and Voss loaded up the cannon with a charge of powder and gunshot. The blast that followed sent the hungry islanders scrambling

A young Norman Luxton (top left) with black bear and other friends.

for cover as the *Tilikum* sailed away with both "long pigs" untouched by foe or fork.

Their worries were far from over, however. The ancient dugout was no match for the fury of the ocean. During a tropical storm, gigantic waves tossed the *Tilikum* like a helpless toy. The boat was lifted onto a coral reef and Luxton was thrown overboard while Captain Voss slept in his cabin. Luxton lay unconscious on the jagged rocks until Voss found him the next morning. Certain that his first mate was dead, Voss began to dig a grave when Luxton unexpectedly regained consciousness. Before long, Luxton's body began to swell to twice its normal size from coral poisoning. In sheer agony, Luxton sailed with Voss to Suva, Fiji, where a local doctor ordered him aboard the first steamship bound for Australia. Captain Voss was left to sail the *Tilikum* into Sydney without his partner. To replace Luxton, Voss took a Tasmanian on as first mate, but shortly after their departure, a fierce storm swept the new first mate and the ship's compass overboard. Both were lost and Voss was forced to continue on his own to Australia.

After 16,000 harrowing kilometres, Luxton decided to end his marine adventure. He remained in Australia to recuperate from his injuries while the fearless Captain Voss faced the elements alone, sailing the *Tilikum* safely around Australia, through the Indian Ocean, around South Africa and ultimately to London, England, where on September 2, 1904, the *Tilikum* voyage finally came to an end. Nine years later, Captain John Voss set sail on a new marine adventure, leaving Yokohama, Japan to cross the Pacific in a yawl. He was never heard from again.

The *Tilikum* was sold in London and remained there for many years, neglected and forgotten, rotting in a ship graveyard on the Thames. Eventually it was recovered, given a fresh coat of paint and returned to the city of Victoria, where it can still be seen, fully restored, on display at the Marine Museum of British Columbia.

As for Norman Luxton, after leaving Australia he returned to his native Canada, and settled in Banff, Alberta, to regain his health. Before long he was ready to embark on a new life adventure. Luxton founded the *Crag and Canyon* newspaper which he published for 49 years. He opened a trading post and became a prominent businessman about town, owning many properties including the Lux Theatre and the King Edward Hotel.

Norman Luxton soon became a household word and was nicknamed "the oracle of Banff." No one contributed more to the town's early development than Luxton. He seemed to be behind every Banff project and tourist event from Winter Carnival to the Annual Indian Days Festival still held every summer. For over 25 years Luxton judged several Native events at the Calgary Stampede. The Stoney First Nations became his good friends and Luxton saw to it that they were treated fairly in all competitions.

When Luxton moved his trading post north to Morley, he proved once more his commitment to the Stoneys. In 1918 a virulent influenza epidemic was killing the Aboriginal population with a vengeance. Luxton wasted no time in organizing immediate burials. He fed the sick from supplies in his own store, giving them whatever he had on hand. He had no knowledge of medicine but in desperation, administered aspirin and whisky to those suffering, never asking for anything in return. Slowly his many "patients" began to recover. His trading post in Morley failed but the Stoneys never forgot his kindness and compassion. The Blackfoot First Nations made Luxton Honorary Chief White Eagle and the Stoneys named him Chief White Shield, believing he could shield them from all harm.

In 1904 Luxton married Georgina McDougall, reportedly the first non-Aboriginal child born in what is now the province of Alberta. Their daughter, Eleanor Luxton, studied mechanical engineering and became a designer for the Canadian Pacific

Railway, but she was more interested in local history and writing. Eleanor would later edit and publish her father's journal describing his marine adventure in her book, *Tilikum, Luxton's Pacific Crossing*.

On October 31, 1962, at the age of 86, Norman Kenny Luxton died. Among the many mourners attending his funeral were his Aboriginal friends, fully attired in ceremonial costume, paying their final respects and bidding farewell to the Honorary Chief.

Norman Luxton's legacy lives on in Banff. Visitors can view his vast collection of local First Nations relics and artifacts at the Luxton Museum, which he founded in his later years as a tribute to the great spirit of *Tilikum*—friendship.

In Pursuit
of Treasure

OAK ISLAND IS ONE OF THREE HUNDRED LITTLE ISLANDS ON NOVA SCOTIA'S SOUTH SHORE ABOUT AN HOUR'S DRIVE SOUTHWEST OF HALIFAX. As tiny as it is, Oak Island is home to one of the world's best kept secrets. Known as "the Money Pit," it has attracted treasure seekers from all walks of life.

The Restall family, setting up the cribbing for the Money Pit.

For over two centuries an ancient maze of underground platforms and booby-trapped flood tunnels have managed to outsmart the most advanced technology. Numerous theories have been presented over the years to explain the mystery, but so far no one knows where the treasure has been buried or even what it is. According to local legend, when the last oak tree has gone from the island and seven men have died seeking the fortune, the treasure will finally be found. The oak trees have now disappeared from Oak Island and to date, six men have died in pursuit of the treasure.

The obsession began in 1795 when 15-year-old Daniel McGinnis, a native of nearby Chester, was exploring some of the islands in Mahone Bay with his friends John Smith and Anthony Vaughan. The boys were attracted to the one and only island in the bay that was covered in tall oak trees and decided to investigate. On the island, they came upon a large oak tree in the middle of a clearing. What remained of a block and tackle dangled from the end of a broken branch which someone had sawed off. Directly below the old pulley system, the boys noticed a circular dip in the ground. It appeared to be a large hole that had been filled with loose soil.

The boys were overjoyed with their discovery. For years stories of pirates and privateers had been told around campfires. Could it be, they wondered, that they had accidentally stumbled upon the burial site of Captain Kidd's legendary treasure? McGinnis, Smith and Vaughan began to dig furiously under the old oak tree. They had dug down a little more than half a metre when they reached a layer of unusual flagstones. After removing the stones, the boys realized that they were entering an old shaft or pit. The sides of the shaft had pick marks and scratches in the hard clay but the earth inside was loose. At a depth of 3 metres their shovels hit wood. Surely they had struck a treasure chest, the boys thought. McGinnis, Smith and Vaughan soon realized, however, that what they had hit was a platform of oak logs. Thinking it couldn't be much longer until they unearthed their prize, the boys continued

Robert Restall descending into the Pit that would take his life.

digging. Day after day McGinnis, Smith and Vaughan returned
to the pit with their picks and shovels. After removing the first
layer of oak logs, they found another depression of loose earth,
followed by another layer of oak logs, another layer of earth,
and at 9 metres, yet another layer of oak logs. By this time the
boys knew they could not continue without special equipment
and more manpower. Unfortunately no one back home was
prepared to get involved in the search. Locals were frightened
by tales of strange lights and mysterious disappearances on the
island.

Eight long years passed before McGinnis, Smith and Vaughan, along with several dozen eager businessmen, formed the Onslow Company and returned to Oak Island. They found that the oak platforms were sealed with a type of cement containing coconut fibres. How did coconut material from the tropics end up on Oak Island? At a depth of 27 metres, a large flat rock with a mysterious inscription carved in the surface was removed from the pit. The inscription would create a controversy that would last for decades as different "authorities" attempted to decode the strange markings.

A few metres below the mysterious rock, the men hit something solid. It felt like wood but was harder than the oak platforms above it. Unfortunately nightfall was approaching and they were forced to wait for daylight. The following morning they returned to the pit eager to resume. Much to their surprise, the entire shaft had filled with water overnight. Despite their frantic efforts, the faster they tried pumping the water out, the faster it filled up again.

The following spring the group tried digging a new shaft close to the first. At 34 metres they changed direction and started to tunnel toward the Money Pit. Without warning, water burst through the walls and flooded the new shaft to the same level as the first. Everyone managed to get out alive, but the Onslow Company had run out of funds and was forced to give up.

Thus began the long procession of companies and investors, one after the other, who would eventually exhaust their funds and admit defeat. The Truro Company decided to use powerful augers to drill deep within the pit. Their augers did manage to bring up 60 centimetres of gold chain, a few loose gold coins and a piece of old parchment paper with writing on it. They also learned that the water in the pit was salty and appeared to rise and fall with the ocean tides. The Truro Company dug other shafts, but sooner or later, each one filled with water.

From 1861 to 1864 the Oak Island Association tried a

different method using high-powered pumps. As they were setting up the first pump, tragedy struck. It exploded without warning, burning one of the men to death. Two other men narrowly escaped with their lives when the bottom of the pit literally dropped out beneath them, leaving the company to conclude that a huge cavern must exist at the bottom of the pit.

In 1893 Frederick Blair formed the Oak Island Treasure Company. Over a six-year period, 16 more shafts were dug. Blair's plan was to explode dynamite along the flood tunnels. Disaster struck when a pulley broke and one of the men plunged to his death. By the time the company ran out of money, so many holes had been drilled that it was impossible to tell which was the original Money Pit.

In 1909 Henry Bowdoin managed to pool together a few interested investors, including a young Franklin D. Roosevelt (who would become the 32nd American president in 1933). Thousands of dollars were spent on the digs but nothing of value was found. Angry and frustrated, Bowdoin declared the Oak Island treasure a hoax.

Time and again, treasure seekers would return to the pit, only to find it filled with water by morning.

The Money Pit continued to attract a wide variety of fortune seekers, but one of the most curious was a motorcycle daredevil from Hamilton, Ontario. Robert Restall and his wife, Mildred, were known for their circus act called the "Globe of Death" which featured the two of them travelling towards each other at speeds over 100 kilometres an hour from opposite directions, along the inside walls of the globe. Robert looped around the top of the globe while Mildred rode across the circle horizontally. Audiences would hold their breath as the two of them narrowly missed each other. Sometimes they did not miss. Mildred once broke her jaw and Robert fractured his arm while performing in Germany.

After 20 years of show business, the Restalls decided to turn to a less dangerous lifestyle. Robert gathered up his life savings and moved his wife and two sons to Oak Island, determined to solve the mystery. For five long years the entire family lived on the island in a primitive shack with no electricity, telephone, running water or toilet. On August 17, 1965, without warning, their dream quest turned into a nightmare.

Robert Restall had been working in one of the shafts when he suddenly disappeared from view. His son, Robert Junior, and five other workers instantly ran to his aid. One by one they climbed down the ladder into the shaft and, one by one, each of them was overcome by something and passed out. Three of the workers lying unconscious at the bottom of the pit were rescued and revived. The other four, including Restall and his son, were beyond reach. Firemen had to pump the pit dry to find their bodies in the murky water. Autopsies later revealed that all four men had died of drowning, but what caused them to lose consciousness and fall was never determined. Many claimed that toxic fumes from the gas pumps had seeped into the pit. Others said it was the curse of Oak Island.

The next, and last company to try to match wits with the Money Pit was the Triton Alliance, established in 1969. On September 16, 1972, a remote-controlled underwater camera was lowered into a shaft named Borehole 10X while Dan

Blankenship, director of operations for Triton, watched on a closed-circuit video monitor in his office. At a depth of 73 metres Blankenship thought he saw what appeared to be three chests in the muddy waters of a large cavern. Suddenly another image appeared on screen—a fleshy human hand severed at the wrist and a body slumped against the wall of the cavern. This vision only served to rekindle speculation of pirate treasure. Pirates were known to bury one of their own along with their treasure to stand guard and protect their loot.

Blankenship has maintained for several years that Borehole 10X, located about 60 metres from the Money Pit, contains the secret to the mystery. He is so convinced, in fact, that he has attempted several dives into the shaft to explore the murky hole himself. On one of his dives he nearly became the island's seventh victim when the sides of the shaft caved in and his air hose kinked, leaving him to surface on one remaining breath.

Triton is planning a massive dig as soon as the company can raise enough money. In 1988 the estimated cost for this venture exceeded $10 million, but the price tag has grown considerably since then. The plan is to sink a huge steel cylinder around the shaft, preventing the sides from collapsing while sealing off the flood tunnels. Triton is certain this will allow divers to get to the bottom of the shaft once and for all.

On the other side of the island lives Fred Nolan. Nolan has made some startling discoveries of his own. While surveying his property he found a striking pattern of stones and boulders serving as markers of some sort. One of the stones was carved in the shape of a human head. Plotting the stones on a graph, Nolan drew a line connecting all the markers and discovered that it formed the shape of a giant Christian cross with the stone head right at the centre. Nolan thinks that the Money Pit was simply an elaborate decoy and the treasure really lies beneath a swamp on his property.

Two centuries have passed since McGinnis, Smith and Vaughan made their fascinating discovery. Architects, archaeologists, engineers, treasure hunters, historians and psychics have all tried to match wits with the genius of the pit. After two hundred years, all that is known is that someone has gone to a great deal of trouble to bury something of tremendous value.

When asked if he has any idea what might be down there, Dan Blankenship simply shakes his head and smiles.

The original site of the Money Pit discovered by McGinnis, Smith and Vaughn.

Part Four

A Different Kind
of Hero

Four Funerals
for Sophia Cameron

NOWHERE IN THE HISTORY OF CANADA IS THERE A MORE POWERFUL STORY OF LOVE AND HONOUR THAN THAT OF CARIBOO CAMERON AND HIS WIFE, SOPHIA. Cariboo Cameron adored his beautiful young wife. When she suddenly became ill, he was shattered. As Cameron kneeled by her bedside watching her slip away, he swore that nothing would prevent him from carrying out her dying wish.

John Angus
"Cariboo" Cameron.

His steely determination proved just how far he was prepared to go to fulfill his promise.

John Angus "Cariboo" Cameron grew up in Glengarry County in Eastern Ontario, not far from the Quebec border. In 1852 at the age of 32, he went west with two brothers to join the California gold rush. After six successful years there the Camerons heard about the discovery of gold on British Columbia's Fraser River and headed north. Once again they seemed blessed with the Midas touch. By the time they decided

Wedding of John Angus "Cariboo" Cameron and Margaret Sophia Groves (second row centre).

to return to their home in Cornwall in 1860, they were twenty thousand dollars richer.

Now a man of means, John Angus, age forty, courted and married his longtime sweetheart, 28-year-old Margaret Sophia Groves. When Cameron learned that gold had been discovered in the Cariboo, he was eager to try his luck again, but Sophia was less than enthusiastic. She had led a comfortable, sheltered life and had serious reservations about embarking on such an exotic adventure. Her husband persuaded her to accompany him to the western goldfields, however, and soon the couple and their four-month-old baby, Alice, were on their way.

In the days before the Trans-Canada Railway, the trip from Cameron's hometown to the west coast involved a gruelling 18,000 kilometre sea voyage in addition to an endless portage through the tropical jungles of Panama. En route baby Alice became sick. By the time the Camerons docked in Victoria ten months after setting out, her condition worsened, and one week later little Alice died. Heartbroken, John and Sophia moved on to the goldfields in the interior along with another Glengarry native, Robert Stevenson, whom they had met in Victoria.

Stevenson and Cameron soon began a business partnership and staked a claim on Williams Creek in the Cariboo near the boomtown of Barkerville. This claim would later become Cariboo Cameron's namesake and his path to fame and fortune. A few weeks later Robert Stevenson transferred his interest in the claim to the Camerons, making them the majority shareholders. The shaft did not pay off at first and with winter rapidly approaching, the miners wondered if they had staked the right location.

There were only twelve women living in the Cariboo at that time. Sophia became involved in her husband's business interests and was the only woman to hold a miner's licence in the Cariboo.

Conditions were harsh and primitive in the Cariboo. The weather was brutal and a typhoid epidemic was rampant in the area. Sophia, pregnant again, longed for the comforts of her parents' farm. She gave birth to a stillborn child and shortly thereafter caught the dreaded typhoid fever. Raging winds howled through their drafty little cabin and Cameron could not keep the place warm as the thermometer outside dipped to 30 degrees below zero. Sophia complained bitterly and begged to go home. The resident doctor was called but Sophia's condition took a sudden turn for the worse. Robert Stevenson, who shared the cabin with them, recalled Sophia's dying words to her husband seated by her side: "John, promise you'll take me home, that you'll never leave my body in this awful place." Cameron vowed to fulfill her wish, not fully comprehending the enormity of the drama that lay before him. At 3:00 a.m., October 23, 1862, Sophia Cameron died.

Her body was wrapped in her favourite shawl, a wedding gift from her sister, and placed in a tin casket fitted inside a wooden coffin. Cameron buried his wife temporarily under an abandoned cabin, vowing to work until he earned enough money to take her home.

Two months later workers at the mine struck it rich, making Cameron one of the wealthiest men in Canada, but his beloved Sophia was not there to share it. Instead, Cameron removed just enough gold dust from the mine to finance the heartbreaking trip back east to honour her final request.

Cameron generously offered $12 a day to anyone willing to help him haul Sophia's coffin to Victoria, where they would receive an additional $2,000 bonus for completing the trip. Twenty-two men accepted the offer, including his good friend Robert Stevenson. The 600 kilometre trek to Victoria would take them through massive snowdrifts, freezing temperatures, uncharted wilderness and dense mountain forests.

Sophia's coffin was placed on a toboggan loaded down with blankets, food and 23 kilograms of gold dust. Cameron walked ahead of the men, cutting the brush to make a path as they pulled the heavy, awkward load. The arduous journey proved to be too difficult for most of the men. At each roadhouse along the way several of them turned back. Cameron was forced to purchase three horses to pull the massive load. By the time he reached the Fraser River, all three horses had died of exhaustion and only his faithful friend and associate, Robert Stevenson, remained.

At Port Douglas they put the coffin onto a steamship and headed out to Victoria, arriving on March 7, 1863. The next day Sophia's tin coffin was filled with alcohol and sealed to preserve her body for the long ocean voyage back to Ontario, but she would not be making the trip yet. Cariboo Cameron had to return to Williams Creek to work his claim or risk losing it, so Sophia was temporarily buried a second time in Victoria.

Cameron and Stevenson returned to the Cariboo in early spring. They worked the mine until October of 1863, removing huge quantities of gold. The Cameron Company claim became the richest in the entire colony. A little town sprang up around the claim just north of Barkerville and was called Cameronton in his honour. John Cameron had finally mined enough of his wealth to fulfill his promise to Sophia.

Cameron, Stevenson and eight horses laden with gold made their way to Victoria. Sophia's coffin was exhumed and loaded onto a ship which would take her back the way she had come, along the entire Pacific coast to Panama, through the tropical jungle portage and then onto another ship headed for New York.

The extraordinary weight of the coffin roused the suspicions of customs officials in New York who thought that Cameron might be using it as a way to smuggle gold into the country. Cameron, determined to protect his wife's dignity, would not allow anyone to open the coffin for inspection, which only increased suspicions. Cameron and Stevenson swore under oath as to the contents of the coffin, but the customs officials were not convinced. After a delay of two weeks, Cameron finally offered to pay the expenses of one customs officer to accompany him and witness the burial in Cornwall. With that he was allowed to continue on his way from New York to Quebec City and finally, by train to Cornwall.

News of Cameron's fantastic gold strike had reached the east long before his arrival. The local newspapers were filled with details of his sudden wealth, but the New York papers seemed more interested in the coffin and Cameron's fight with the authorities. Canadian papers quickly picked up on this and before long, rumours began to circulate that Sophia was not dead at all. Gossip mongers claimed that she was still very much alive and that her husband had sold her into slavery, faking her death in order to secretly smuggle some of his gold out of Barkerville in her coffin. Speculation grew until some citizens of the town demanded to have the coffin opened, which Cameron flatly refused to do. In December of 1863 Sophia was given a proper burial, her third, and laid to rest in the family plot in Cornwall as she had requested. Cameron's promise was finally fulfilled, but the story was far from over.

In spite of the controversy, Cariboo Cameron decided to settle in the area. He bought a large farm in nearby Summerstown and built a mansion on the property. He then proceeded to share his wealth with his family. Two brothers were each given $20,000; two other brothers (who had accompanied and helped him in Barkerville) were each given $40,000 and a farm.

In 1865, three years after Sophia's death, Cameron remarried. His second wife, Christina Adelaide Wood, was the daughter of his distinguished neighbour, Colonel Wood. She was 21 years his junior. For a while they lived well in Fairfield House, his stone mansion in Summerstown. Eventually however, the old rumours began to resurface. At the time of Sophia's burial Cameron had refused to respond to the gossip in town, but now accusations that Sophia was still alive raised suspicions of bigamy.

Out of respect for his new wife, Cameron decided to put an end to the rumours once and for all. In 1873 he sent notices to the town authorities and to Sophia's family that he planned to raise her coffin one last time. Several hundred curiosity-seekers came to witness the event as a tinsmith cut open the casket and drained out the alcohol. Sophia's parents looked with sadness at their lost child, perfectly preserved before them. Her sister burst into tears as she recognized the shawl she had given Sophia on her wedding day.

Disgusted by the whole ordeal, Cameron refused to have her reburied in Cornwall. The coffin was resealed and taken to the cemetery in nearby Summerstown where Sophia was laid to rest for the fourth and final time.

Despite his fabulous wealth, the fates were not kind to Cariboo Cameron. He became involved in a number of risky

Final resting place of Sophia Cameron, in the Salem United Church cemetery.

Grave of Cariboo Cameron in Cameronton, BC.

ventures which failed one after another. In 1886 he decided that the only way to recoup his lost fortune was to try his luck again at what he knew best—mining in the mountains of central B.C.

Cariboo Cameron and his wife Christina returned to the Cariboo, taking the trip he knew all too well. An older, weaker Cameron tried prospecting once more, but twenty-four years had passed since his lucky strike in the B.C. goldfields and everything had changed. Cameron moved back to B.C. the old boom-town of Barkerville where he died two years later, a poor and broken man. He was buried in the little Cameronton cemetery. Few people from the town which bore his name came to pay their last respects. Christina Cameron lived to the age of 87 and died peacefully in Montreal.

In its heyday Barkerville was the largest town west of Chicago and north of San Francisco. Today all that remains of the little gold rush town is a living museum a short walk away from the historic cemetery in Cameronton. Cariboo Cameron's stone mansion, Fairfield House, still stands in Summerstown, Ontario. According to legend, the grass never grew on the spot in the Cornwall cemetery where the alcohol had been spilled from Sophia's coffin.

Cariboo Cameron's pioneer spirit helped create a town, but his greatest legacy was the extraordinary sacrifice he made in the name of love.

Above and Beyond
the Call of Duty

IN MANY WAYS HIS COMRADES THOUGHT OF HIM AS A TYPICAL SOLDIER. He liked spending time with the troops, never complained much about the food, enjoyed an occasional beer and was quite a hit with the ladies. Good old Billy was a grisly sort of fellow with his scruffy beard and hammertoes, but the army didn't seem to mind.

Sergeant Bill in action near the front lines during World War I.

Today he looks rather handsome in his regimental blue cape decorated with the Fifth Battalion Badge, his sergeant's chevrons, five service stripes and a wound stripe. His medals— the 1914 Mons Star, the General Service Medal and the Victory Medal—tell of his bravery at the front.

Bill suffered all the horrors of the Great War. He was gassed in battle, received a shrapnel wound to the neck, developed trench foot and was shell-shocked, yet he held his own from Neuve Chappelle to Passchendaele. Everyone in the 5th Battalion, Canadian Expeditionary Force said Sergeant Bill was a hero through and through—except for one minor technicality. Sergeant Bill was a goat.

On August 23, 1914, the Fighting Fifth, Western Cavalry (also known as the Red Saskatchewans) stopped at Broadview, Saskatchewan, a small town about a two hour drive east of Regina. At the time, Billy Goat was Daisy Curwain's special pet. Daisy's father Fred had bought the goat for his daughter and managed to train the clever animal to pull a cart and a sleigh. When the troops saw the goat they made quite a fuss over the unsuspecting Billy. With Daisy's permission Mr. Curwain presented his daughter's pet to the Fighting Fifth. Daisy assured them that he would bring them luck, and so Private Bill was enlisted with the Western Cavalry as their mascot.

Off he went aboard the CPR to Valcartier, a camp in Quebec. Somehow the boys managed to get the goat onto the *S.S. Lapland* bound for England. The transatlantic voyage was difficult and long. Bill got seasick along with the best of them but on the morning of October 20, 1914, they arrived in Plymouth, England, where Bill was ordered into quarantine. Once again the boys came to his rescue and hid Bill before he could be taken away. They smuggled him out of England and into France where they arrived at the front on February 15, 1915. By the following spring Bill was in the trenches near Armentiers.

It was not long before Private Bill once again found himself in a tight spot. This time he had no one to blame but himself when he was caught poking about in the Orderly Room, where he ate the Battalion Nominal Role. Remnants of the Role were later found in his barracks. A few days later Bill charged a superior officer. Two arrests in one month put Bill's army career in serious jeopardy. There was talk of a discharge. Rumours circulated that Private Bill was a traitor or possibly a German spy.

Fortunately Bill was able to redeem himself a short while later at the battle of Neuve Chapelle, where his quick actions saved the lives of Sergeant William Rae and two other soldiers. Goats, like most animals, have a highly developed sense of hearing. During a time of intense shelling by the Germans, Bill must have heard the familiar high-pitched whistle and sensed what was about to happen. He immediately butted the sergeant and the other two men into the trenches seconds before the shells exploded. For this act of heroism Bill was promoted to the rank of sergeant.

After his promotion Sergeant Bill had a special place of honour among his men. Whenever the troops changed location he could be seen riding proud, high atop a transport truck, attracting much attention and lifting the spirits of many war-weary soldiers en route.

Sergeant Bill proved himself again during the second battle of Ypres where he was gassed. Then in Festhubert, Bill was found standing over a Prussian guard in spite of the fact that he was bleeding from a shrapnel wound to the neck.

In December of 1915 Sergeant Bill developed trench foot, or more accurately, trench hoof, at Hill 63. Two years later in April of 1917, he was shell-shocked at Hill 70 during the battle of Vimy Ridge and was wounded twice by shrapnel at Festhubert. In addition to these horrors, Sergeant Bill went missing in August of 1918 and was charged with being AWOL. The troops feared that their mascot might have fallen into the hands of the Bengal Lancers who were known to enjoy the taste of goat meat, but Bill returned unharmed. Where he went and what occurred remains a mystery, though some said he had been captured by enemy forces and managed to escape.

On November 11, 1918—at the eleventh hour of the eleventh day of the eleventh month—orders arrived to cease fire. The war was over but another battle raged for Sergeant Bill. How were the men going to get the old goat home? They were determined to see Sergeant Bill demobilized and returned to Canada along with them but the authorities in England had a different idea. They would not allow Sergeant Bill to board the ship for home. The men presented a strong case for Bill, citing his many acts of bravery and heroism. Under no circumstances would they leave him behind. An excerpt from the diary of Vic Swanston of the Fighting Fifth says it best: "That mascot came from the west with us, went through the whole damn war at the Front, was gassed at the Second Battle of Ypres, wounded by shrapnel at Festhubert and is going back, in spite of hell and high water and the whole British Army and Navy."

Sergeant Bill arrived in Canada on April 19, 1919, after four and a half years of active duty overseas. Canadian immigration officers, however, refused to allow the goat into the country. Once again the troops came to his defence. Sergeant Bill was granted entry and returned to Broadview, leading his battalion down the main street in the victory parade.

Later that week he was taken to see his former owner, Daisy Curwain, no longer a little girl. Much had changed during Bill's absence. Daisy's family had relocated and were not able to take him back. Sergeant Bill ended up in Regina where he lived until his death later that year.

His friends from the Fighting Fifth were saddened by his passing and vowed not to let their mascot be forgotten. They arranged to have Bill's body preserved by the Museum of Natural History. Sergeant Bill was put on display in the Provincial Museum in Regina, and later in the Legislative Library where he remained from 1929 to 1936. He was then moved to the Plains Historical Museum where he spent several years before being put away in storage, ragged and moth-eaten.

In 1980 the people of Broadview petitioned to have Sergeant Bill brought home. He was returned to the Broadview Historical Museum where they arranged to have him cleaned and restored to his former glory by the Canadian Conservation Institute. Today Sergeant Bill can be seen proudly wearing his gold tassels draped elegantly on his horns. His new medals, replacing the originals which had been stolen—the 1914 Mons Star, The General Service Medal and the Victory Medal—are displayed before him. Sergeant Bill stands beside a statue of a World War I soldier, front and centre in the Broadview Museum, lest we forget the men and mascot of the Great War.

Sergeant Bill and his medals on permanent display in Saskatchewan's Broadview Museum.

Godmother
to the West

WHEN MARIE-ANNE GABOURY WAS A YOUNG GIRL GROWING UP IN THE LITTLE TOWN OF MASKINONGÉ NEAR QUEBEC CITY, SHE PICTURED A TYPICAL HABITANT LIFE FOR HERSELF. Like all young girls in the late 1700s, she was expected to settle down, marry a farmer and have a large family. Marie-Anne never dreamed that she would be the first Canadian woman of European descent to lead the dangerous life of a voyageur and settle in the North West, but that is exactly what happened when she fell in love and married Jean-Baptiste Lagimodière. In time she produced such a large family that the Salteaux First Nations named her "Ningah," meaning "Mother." Not only did she have eight children of her own, but as the only Christian non-Native woman among them, she became godmother to over a hundred Aboriginal and Métis children from Manitoba to Alberta. Marie-Anne also lived to watch her grandson Louis Riel become the "Father of Manitoba" and lead the province into Confederation.

At the age of twelve Marie-Anne became a housekeeper serving at the home of the parish priest in Maskinongé. A quiet, religious girl, she remained there until she met Jean-Baptiste Lagimodière, a charming young fur trader who was visiting his family after five years in Canada's North West. When Lagimodière asked for her hand in marriage, Marie-Anne was delighted, assuming that he had returned to settle down and farm like all the other young men she had known. Shortly after their marriage in the spring of 1806, however, Jean-Baptiste announced that the North West was calling him again. He was too restless to settle down to a life of farming. Marie-Anne told her husband that wherever he went, she would go. At first Jean-Baptiste protested, stating that no woman had ever travelled in a voyageur's canoe. It simply was not done. Jean-Baptiste did not know his wife well enough at the time to understand her incredible determination. After all arguments were exhausted, he finally gave in, warning Marie-Anne not to expect any special treatment or privileges.

A brigade of canoes left Lachine near Montreal and headed west. There were 18 men in each canoe keeping up a steady rhythm of 50 strokes per minute from dawn to dusk. Marie-Anne did not have to paddle but she was placed in charge of all the cooking and sewing. The trip from Montreal to Lake Huron was extremely difficult but the voyageurs arrived without incident or casualties. Once they reached Lake Superior, however, they encountered storms unlike any they had ever seen. One of the canoes in their expedition capsized, drowning the entire crew. By the time the voyageurs reached Fort William (now Thunder Bay), near the western tip of Lake Superior, they had completed 36 portages. Marie-Anne carried her own massive bag of personal belongings without complaint though she was in the early stages of her first pregnancy.

In late summer of 1806 the voyageurs arrived in Pembina, North Dakota, a Métis encampment on the Canadian border, to spend the winter. If Marie-Anne thought her life would be less eventful for the next few months, she was mistaken. The Lagimodières were quickly forced to travel farther upriver to escape a jealous and angry Native woman—Jean-Baptiste's common-law wife. Jean-Baptiste had lived with the woman for five years during his earlier travels and she was not about to share him with Marie-Anne.

When it was safe the couple returned to the fort at Pembina in January of 1807 where their first child, Reine, was born. For the next five months Marie-Anne and baby Reine were alone most of the time while Jean-Baptiste was off hunting. When spring arrived the Lagimodières set out in a canoe and headed north along with three other voyageurs (Chalifou, Belgrade and Paquin) and their Cree wives.

For the next four years the group spent the winters in the Fort of the Prairies (now Edmonton). Marie-Anne could not speak the Cree language but she was grateful for the company of women. When the fur season was over the four men would leave the safety of the Fort to go buffalo hunting on the Prairies. They lived a nomadic existence, pitching their tents wherever the hunt led them.

Unfortunately, Marie-Anne's silent friendship with the Aboriginal women was short-lived. While the men were away hunting, the Scarcees, who hated the Cree, used the opportunity to get their revenge. Finding the women alone and unprotected, they stormed the tents and massacred the Cree women. Only Marie-Anne was spared.

Perhaps the most hair-raising encounter of Marie-Anne's life occurred the very next day. After packing up, the group headed back to the Fort. Marie-Anne followed on horseback with little Reine tucked into a moss bag hanging off the side of her horse. Suddenly a herd of buffalo crossed their path spooking Marie-Anne's horse. It took off in pursuit of the herd with Marie-Anne hanging on for dear life and baby Reine in her moss bag flapping wildly against the horse's side. Jean-Baptiste chased after them but it took some time for his horse to catch up and control the runaway. Marie-Anne, shaking and exhausted from the ordeal, finally stepped down unharmed. The men pitched a tent near some trees and a few hours later Marie-Anne gave birth to her second child, whom she and Jean-Baptiste nicknamed Laprairie.

The little boy was a pretty baby with exceptionally white skin, fair hair and blue eyes. His unusual colouring attracted a great deal of attention from the locals. One Blackfoot woman attempted to kidnap him but was stopped by Marie-Anne just before escaping the village. On another occasion an Assiniboine chief offered Marie-Anne a fine horse in exchange for her son. When she refused he increased his offer to two and then five horses. Realizing she still wasn't impressed, the chief offered one of his own children in exchange for the blond, blue-eyed boy. Marie-Anne fell to her knees and began to cry so hysterically that the chief finally turned and left.

In 1811 Jean-Baptiste learned that Lord Selkirk was establishing a colony on the banks of the Red River near present-day Winnipeg. The couple, now with three children, left the Plains to settle near the junction of the Red and Assiniboine Rivers.

Conflict erupted in 1815 between the North West Company and the Hudson's Bay Company (H.B.C.), which had been established in the area for years. The H.B.C. turned to Jean-Baptiste for help. Someone had to inform Lord Selkirk in Montreal that the Company was in trouble. It was a dangerous mission through enemy lines but Jean-Baptiste was their only hope. In November of that year, entirely on his own with nothing but a small canoe and a few provisions, Jean-Baptiste set out along the familiar 2,900 kilometre route of the voyageurs, carrying the emergency dispatch to Lord Selkirk. Marie-Anne and the children stayed behind in the relative safety of Fort Douglas (Winnipeg).

Jean-Baptiste arrived in Montreal in record time. Lord Selkirk was so impressed—and grateful—he invited him to stay and rest awhile but Jean-Baptiste was anxious to return to his family. On his way home he was captured by the North West Company and taken prisoner. Jean-Baptiste was held for several months at Fort William. Marie-Anne was certain that her husband had met with tragedy on such a perilous voyage but she had her own worries in Fort Douglas. Hostilities were increasing between the two rival companies with each one launching attacks on the other's forts. Shortly before the North West Company attacked Fort Douglas, Chief Peguis of the Salteaux took Marie-Anne and her children into his camp across the river away from danger. She and the children spent the summer and fall in the Chief's tepee but as winter approached, Marie-Anne sought a warmer place to stay. She found an old abandoned cabin nearby where she and her children lived for three months never knowing if they would perish in the freezing weather. Jean-Baptiste had been gone 14 months and Marie-Anne was beginning to accept her fate when a haggard man in ragged clothes, badly in need of a shave, appeared unexpectedly at her cabin door. Jean-Baptiste had returned.

A few days later Lord Selkirk's soldiers arrived and recaptured Fort Douglas. As a reward for his heroism Lord Selkirk gave Jean-Baptiste a large tract of land on the bank of the Red River. Realizing that religion would stabilize the community, Lord Selkirk sent for two priests from Quebec. By the time the priests arrived, there was a lineup of a hundred or more Aboriginal and Métis children waiting to be baptized. Marie-Anne became godmother to each and every one of them.

Jean-Baptiste decided to settle the land he was given but he and his family suffered great personal hardship. It had been 12 years since Marie-Anne had eaten a piece of bread and she could hardly wait for her first wheat harvest. But plague after plague of grasshoppers and mice infested the fields, and for five years the residents nearly starved.

Marie-Anne and Jean-Baptiste eventually had a total of eight children. On September 7, 1855, at the age of 76, Jean-Baptiste died. Marie-Anne spent the next twenty years in the home of her son, Benjamin. She died on December 14, 1875, at the age of 95, surrounded by all her children and grandchildren. She lived long enough to watch her grandson Louis Riel, son of Julie Lagimodière, rise to fame and power in Manitoba. Fortunately Marie-Anne never knew of his political fall from grace and died before his controversial execution.

Louis Riel addressing a packed Regina, Saskatchewan court house, 1885.

Louis Riel.

Cemetetry in Batoche, Saskatchewan, site of the final battle between the Metis and government troops.

Monument and gravestone of Louis Riel, famous grandson of Marie-Anne Gaboury.

The Mightiest Man
in the World

LOUIS CYR, CANADA'S MOST FAMOUS STRONGMAN, BECAME A LEGEND IN HIS OWN LIFETIME. Nearly a century has passed since his death yet his name is still revered in sporting circles. In his native Quebec where much of the rural wealth was derived from farms and lumber camps, muscular strength and endurance were valuable assets and Louis Cyr was considered a hero. He was a Hercules of a man whose showmanship and feats of strength dazzled audiences in North America and Europe. Billed as "the Strongest Man Who Ever Lived," Cyr never backed away from a challenge and remained undefeated throughout his lifetime. He was a man of many talents—he even found time to play the violin—but it was his massive physique and superhuman strength that helped make him a household name in the Western world.

When Louis Cyr's parents were expecting their first child, people in the little farming community of St. Cyprien de Napierville, Quebec, southeast of Montreal, knew it would be a big one—especially if the child took after his mother. Monsieur Cyr, a poor Acadian farmer, was a man of average height and weight but his wife was another matter. The powerful 118-kilogram woman, who stood over 183 cm tall, was often seen carrying massive sacks of flour that large, muscular men would not even attempt to lift. On October 10, 1863, the first of the seventeen Cyr children was born tipping the scales at 8 kilograms. He was baptized Noe-Cyprien but was later called Louis.

Louis Cyr: "The Strongest Man Who Ever Lived."

Strength seems to have been a trademark of the Cyr family. Louis's paternal grandfather, Pierre Cyr, had made a name for himself as a strongman in the region, as had his great grandfather, a robust farmer who lived to the age of 102.

Grandpa Cyr was a major influence on little Louis, encouraging the child to develop great physical strength by eating enormous quantities of food and performing rigorous daily exercises. The husky nine-year-old practised by moving and lifting heavy logs and rocks and was often seen carrying calves on his back. By the time he was eleven, Louis weighed over 64 kilograms and was able to defeat grown men at arm-wrestling.

The arrival of one Cyr baby after another put a tremendous financial strain on the household budget. At the age of 12, Louis was forced to find a job to help support the family. He found work as a lumberjack, holding his own with any of the adult men in the camp.

Three years later Louis moved with his family to Lowell, Massachusetts, where he worked at a variety of odd jobs and became proficient in English. Despite a serious bout of typhoid fever and a weight loss of 32 kilograms, he soon regained his health and returned to his previous weight and strength. Before long Cyr was again attracting public attention with his superhuman feats. During a country fair held in Boston, Cyr lifted a horse on his shoulders and proceeded to carry it around the ring to the amazement of onlookers.

At 19 Cyr courted and married Melina Comtois. Next to her new husband the petite young girl was a virtual featherweight at 55 kilograms. The couple moved back to their native Quebec where Louis was challenged by Canadian strongman David Michaud to a boulder-lifting contest. Michaud was eager to have a go at his rival for two reasons. Cyr not only threatened Michaud's athletic reputation, he had married the girl Michaud had been courting. Unfortunately for Michaud it was no contest. Cyr heaved a 220-kilogram boulder which Michaud was unable to budge.

Following this victory Cyr began to tour his home province and later, several New England states, demonstrating his physical prowess. Before weightlifting became a regulated sport the careers of theatrical strongmen such as Louis Cyr were as enthusiastically followed as our modern-day movie stars or rock musicians. Audiences crammed into crowded exhibition sites to see him perform but Cyr's crooked tour manager pocketed most of the profits. Cyr received little compensation for his time and effort. He and wife Melina abandoned the tour leaving the dishonest manager to face an angry crowd of ticket holders.

Back at home Cyr gave up travelling for a while to be with his wife during her pregnancy. After a brief stint on the Montreal Police Force, Cyr signed on with a legitimate tour promoter and began making serious money. Before long the Cyrs were safely out of debt, but fortune did not smile kindly upon the young couple. They lost their infant son shortly after his birth.

By 1889 Louis Cyr's reputation and fame spread to distant audiences when his manager arranged a triumphant 23-month tour of England. The highlight of Cyr's trip was an invitation to perform before the Prince of Wales. London's Royal Aquarium Theatre was filled to capacity for the event. Five thousand spectators watched as the Canadian strongman lifted a 250-kilogram weight attached to a hook with just one finger. Then with just one hand, he lifted a barrel of cement weighing 142 kilograms to his shoulder. To thundering applause, Cyr backed under a platform weighing over 1,800 kilograms and raised it on his back as he straightened his knees.

At a luncheon given in his honour, the Marquis of Queensbury arranged a contest for Cyr. He offered to hitch his driving horses, one to each of Cyr's arms, and if Cyr could hold them to a standstill, he could claim one of the horses as his own. Cyr, who could never resist a challenge, accepted. At the given signal the horses tried to pull away in opposite directions, but they were unable to move as Cyr held them firmly in place. Cyr returned home to Canada with his prize. For many years he could be seen proudly driving the nobleman's horse through the streets of Montreal.

Undoubtedly Louis Cyr's most outrageous feat of superhuman strength occurred in Boston in 1895. Spectators were dumbfounded when Cyr invited eighteen of the heaviest men in the audience to stand on a plank. Cyr put his back and shoulders under the platform and lifted it up into the air. The combined weight of the plank and the men totalled a record-setting 1,972 kilograms.

Throughout the 1890s Cyr toured across Canada, the United States and Europe. Weightlifting was not yet a standardized sport and many of his stunts were performed as circus acts during his travels with the Ringling Brothers and Barnum and Bailey. The circus was truly a suitable atmosphere for Cyr, who was a natural showman. Cyr would appear on stage wearing a revealing tight-fitting costume and sporting a long hairdo. Members of the crowd were invited to come up on stage and Cyr twirled them in the air while they held onto nothing but his long locks. Even his wife got into the act. Melina once sat nervously atop a ladder that was balanced on her husband's chin. Yet the delicate, diminutive Mrs. Cyr grew accustomed to her husband's theatrics. Between tours the Cyrs lived in Montreal where they owned and operated a popular tavern on Notre Dame Street. To entertain his customers Louis would often toss enormous beer kegs into the air or lift his wife over the bar on the palm of his hand.

Years of excessive eating (it was nothing for Cyr to consume six steaks at a sitting) coupled with the physical demands of his superhuman performances eventually eroded Cyr's health. While working for Barnum he began to lose weight. Cyr appeared visibly tired and his internal organs started to deteriorate. The 37-year-old champion was suffering from heart problems, asthma and severe kidney inflammation. In 1899 Cyr returned to Montreal considerably weakened but his competitive spirit was still alive and well. In 1906, at the age of

43, he challenged his last rival, Hector Decarie, 12 years his junior. Cyr knew he was in failing health but he tried his best against the much younger competitor. The match was ruled a draw but in a gesture of sportsmanship, Cyr raised Decarie's arm and declared him the winner, relinquishing his title as the "Strongest Man in the World."

On November 10, 1912, Louis Cyr died of Bright's disease (a severe kidney ailment). He was 49. News of his death spread far and wide as all of Quebec mourned the loss of their hero. Hundreds of people poured into Montreal to attend the funeral. This amazing Canadian whose feats of strength were larger than life, slipped into immortality, and folklore, as the mightiest man in the world.

Titanic Lifeboat Number 6

WHEN THE WHITE STAR LINE'S "QUEEN OF THE OCEAN" HIT AN ICEBERG IN THE NORTH ATLANTIC ON APRIL 14, 1912, NONE OF ITS PASSENGERS TRULY BELIEVED THE MIGHTY *TITANIC* WOULD FOUNDER. IT WAS, AFTER ALL, UNSINKABLE. The cry for "women and children first" provided numerous opportunities for displays of chivalry and courage but not all the men on board would go down in history as heroes. Although some men were needed to row the lifeboats away from the listing ship, once they were safely adrift, many of these men faced the silent stares and accusations of the women in their lifeboats. How dare they live when so many husbands, sons, fathers and brothers perished in the freezing waters.

Among the 2,200 passengers and crew on the *Titanic*, 25 were Canadian. The upper deck was swarming with the rich and famous, happy to pay $4,320 for a first-class ticket. One of the millionaires on board was Major Arthur Peuchen of Toronto, president of the Standard Chemical Company and a commissioned officer in the Queen's Own Rifles. He was also a lumber tycoon who owned forest reserves near Hinton, Alberta. Major Peuchen was a talkative, pompous man with a tall, athletic build and a commanding presence. Accustomed to making the transatlantic voyage in the finest style, the Major was familiar with the sea captains of his era. The *Titanic*'s maiden voyage was Peuchen's fortieth ocean crossing and although he was pleased with the luxurious fittings of the ocean liner, he was less than impressed with its captain,

Major Arthur Peuchen, controversial Titanic *survivor.*

Edward John Smith. Captain Smith was 62 years of age—far too old a man for the job, according to Peuchen. Smith was known as a society captain, more interested in entertaining his first-class passengers than spending time on the bridge. Major Peuchen voiced his opinions about the captain on several occasions though he later claimed no criticism was intended.

Peuchen was an experienced seaman in his own right. He had crossed the Atlantic in his luxury yacht, the *Vreda*, a 20-metre vessel that had won more races than any other in its class in Canada. The *Vreda*'s success earned Peuchen a lifetime membership in the Royal Canadian Yacht Club where he served as both vice and rear commodore.

Peuchen's other successes were in business. Under his leadership the Standard Chemical Company discovered a new method of extracting acetic acid, acetone and wood alcohol from wood scraps left behind by lumber companies. By 1912 Peuchen's company had factories in Sault Ste. Marie, Fenelon Falls, Thornbury, Parry Sound and Mont Tremblant. Standard Chemical supplied the War Office with acetone for the manufacture of explosives and shipped crude alcohols to refineries in Europe. With a world war looming on the horizon, the Major found himself spending more and more time in England. He had hoped to be back home in Toronto by April 18 to celebrate his 53rd birthday with his wife and children.

The home he was to return to at 599 Jarvis Street was one of the more modest mansions in the neighbourhood, but the true symbol of Peuchen's wealth was a showpiece estate on Lake Simcoe called Woodlands. Woodlands consisted of an enormous wooden home sitting on prime real estate, complete with tennis courts, a golf course, a lawn-bowling green and a marina full of boats.

Peuchen was a seasoned traveller and chose his cabin aboard the *Titanic* more for comfort than for show. Room 104 on the C-Deck was a basic first-class cabin with no porthole or private bath but it was large enough for Peuchen and his possessions—his clothes and jewellery, some gifts for his wife and children and a tin box containing $217,000 in stocks and bonds.

On that fateful evening of April 14, 1912, Peuchen had finished dinner with some friends and was getting ready for bed when he felt an unusual vibration in his cabin. At first he thought a giant wave had struck the ship, but it had been calm when he turned in. Peuchen decided to investigate. As he approached the grand stairway he was told that the ship had struck an iceberg. Peuchen immediately went to the upper deck to see for himself.

By the time he returned for a second look about fifteen minutes later, Peuchen realized that the ship was listing. His worst fears were confirmed when he saw the grim-faced stewards telling people to put on life preservers and get into the lifeboats. Peuchen's first concern was for a sick friend of his, Hugo Ross, who was resting in his cabin. When Ross received the news he declared it would take more than an iceberg to get him out of bed.

So Peuchen quickly returned to his cabin and began changing out of his evening clothes. He donned some heavy underclothing, a shirt, a pair of pants, an old sweater and boots. Then he put on his overcoat and life jacket, leaving his jewellery and the tin box containing his valuable stocks and bonds behind.

On the port side of the deck Peuchen found Captain Smith and Second Officer Charles Lightoller standing next to four lifeboats. The covers had been removed but not the masts or sails. Boats were second nature to the Major. He jumped into one of them and cut the lashings, removing the mast and sail. There was a call for women and children to get into the lifeboats but many refused to leave the comfort of the ship.

By 12:55 a.m. Peuchen and Officer Lightoller had loaded just 20 women and 2 crewmen into lifeboat number 6, though it could hold 60 passengers or more. The lifeboat was being lowered when Quartermaster Hitchens, the crewman in charge of the boat, called up that he could not manage with only one other seaman aboard. With no crewmen in sight Major Peuchen offered to assist. He told Second Officer Lightoller that he was an experienced yachtsman and could help the two men handle the lifeboat. Captain Smith suggested that Peuchen go one deck below and break a window on the promenade to reach the suspended lifeboat. Instead, in a sudden show of bravery, Peuchen shouted to the crewman in lifeboat 6 to throw him the end of the rope from the lowering device. The nearly 53-year-old Major grabbed hold of the rope and dropped down 18 metres in the blackness of night, then lowered himself another 8 metres into the lifeboat. It was an act of sheer daring that might not have been attempted by a man half his age and would go down as Peuchen's finest moment.

It was an odd group of frightened souls sitting in lifeboat number 6. The quartermaster Robert Hitchens had been at the wheel of the *Titanic* when it hit the iceberg, and the other seaman in the lifeboat, Fred Fleet, had been on lookout and had spotted the iceberg. One of the other passengers was Margaret Brown, later known as the "unsinkable Molly Brown," wife of a Denver millionaire.

As soon as Major Peuchen climbed into the boat, Quartermaster Hitchens made certain no one would question his authority. He barked his orders at Peuchen telling him to sit next to Fred Fleet and start rowing immediately. Hitchens was afraid that the suction caused by the sinking ship would pull them all under. After a few minutes of rowing, Peuchen suggested that one of the women should steer so that Hitchens could join the men at the oars, but Hitchens exploded, reminding Peuchen who was in charge of the lifeboat.

By this time water had begun washing over the *Titanic*'s deck and Captain Smith called out for lifeboat number 6 to return to the sinking ship for more passengers. Quartermaster Hitchens, swearing profusely, ignored the captain's command saying, "It's our lives now, not theirs." Peuchen, who had been firmly put in his place earlier by the quartermaster, sat in silence. Later he would report that he knew he was completely powerless to take action. Molly Brown, however, had had enough of Hitchens. She firmly told him to shut up and go back. When he refused, she picked up an oar and began rowing herself, convincing other women to do the same. All the while Peuchen sat in the lifeboat watching the *Titanic* rise high in the air and then plunge suddenly into the ocean. The terrible cries for help in the darkness would echo in Peuchen's memory for the rest of his life.

Once again the women pleaded to go back and rescue some of the passengers in the water, but Hitchens coldly replied there would be nothing but "stiffs" out there. The women became hysterical, knowing that some of those "stiffs" were their loved ones, but Hitchens showed no compassion. The only one to challenge his rule was the unsinkable Molly Brown. It soon became obvious that she had assumed the leadership role among the passengers in the lifeboat. She saved many of them from hypothermia by making sure that everyone had a chance to row and keep warm.

When the survivors were picked up by the S.S. *Carpathia*, Major Peuchen cleverly sought out *Titanic* officer Lightoller on board. He feared that the men who had left the *Titanic* would become social outcasts back home. Peuchen asked Officer Lightoller to sign an affidavit which stated that the officer had ordered him to man lifeboat number 6.

Peuchen had reason to worry about being socially disgraced. People were already questioning how he had managed to escape while so many others remained trapped on the sinking ship. Major Peuchen quickly became a common topic of discussion in Toronto social circles.

Of the survivors, many were too shocked or grief-stricken to speak, but not Major Peuchen. From the moment he stepped off the *Carpathia* onto land, Peuchen had his statement carefully prepared, accusing Captain Smith of "gross carelessness." Peuchen repeated the accusation during countless interviews, adding that the captain had no business dining in the saloon when he knew the ship was passing through an icefield. Peuchen went on to say that he himself had a clear conscience. He claimed it was only his training as a yachtsman that saved him, declaring to the press that he was no coward. The press in return, stated that Peuchen talked too much.

It did not really matter. Few people believed Peuchen's public statements. Speculation ran wild and a rumour circulated that he had cross-dressed in women's clothing in order to get into a lifeboat.

Major Peuchen appeared before the U.S. Senate sub-committee on Tuesday, April 23, 1912, the only Canadian to do so. He stated that he had come to satisfy the requests of "those poor women who came off our boat," claiming they wanted him to tell the court of inquiry what he had seen. Not once during his testimony did Major Peuchen ever mention the name or contribution of Molly Brown.

On May 21, 1912, Arthur Peuchen was relieved to receive his promotion to Lieutenant Colonel from the Queen's Own Rifles. In 1914 with the outbreak of World War I, Peuchen retired from the Standard Chemical Company and led the Home Battalion of the Queen's Own during the first year of the war. He remained in London until the war ended in 1919 but it was not enough to erase the stigma of surviving the *Titanic* disaster.

Peuchen lost much of his fortune in the 1920s as a result of bad investments and was forced to sell his magnificent Lake Simcoe estate. Eventually he left Ontario and moved into his company's dormitory in Hinton, Alberta. Peuchen continued to defend his actions for the rest of his days, claiming that few men would have done what he did, dropping 18 metres at the end of a rope. That may be true, but once inside the lifeboat, why did the Major not help Molly Brown return to those in the water who were crying for help?

Major Peuchen died in Toronto on December 7, 1929, at the age of 69 and was buried in Mount Pleasant Cemetery. Six years after Peuchen's death, Officer Lightoller published his memoirs in which he wrote that Major Peuchen had been unfairly criticized for doing his duty and carrying out a direct order aboard the *Titanic*.

Only two of the twenty lifeboats returned to those poor lost souls freezing to death in the North Atlantic. Lifeboat number 6 was not one of them. Arthur Peuchen was labelled a hero by some, a coward by others. Perhaps he was simply a man who saw the great ship go down—and lived to tell about it.

The Great Farini

**WILLIAM LEONARD HUNT WAS BORN IN 1838 TO
CANADIAN PARENTS LIVING IN LOCKPORT, NEW YORK.**
The Hunts lived a quiet, conservative life in the little American
town just a day's ride from Niagara Falls.

The Great Farini, daredevil.

Mr. Hunt, a humourless man who became the town's mayor, tried to teach his son the "correct" social attitudes and respectable behaviour of a proper gentleman. Much to his parents' disappointment, it seemed that young William was born to be a rebel. Despite his academic and athletic talents, William was always getting into trouble. He would make his mark by doing the most daring, outrageous things imaginable, ultimately making a mockery of his father's quest for respectability.

At the age of five William moved with his family back to southern Ontario, settling in Bowmanville, near Port Hope. Young William found life in the little Victorian community terribly dull and boring, except when the circus came to town. Then William came alive and dreamed of great adventures and exotic places. Copying the circus acts, he taught himself to swing from a barnyard trapeze. He learned how to walk a high wire and began lifting homemade weights to build up his muscles like the strongmen he had seen. Naturally his parents were mortified but, by the time their son was 16, William was already an accomplished amateur performer.

His father tried everything to lure William away from the disgrace of the circus and for a while he succeeded. William was apprenticed to a doctor in the hope that the intelligent young man would learn an honourable profession, but during one of his father's trips to England, William received an offer he could not refuse. The 21-year-old, soon-to-be doctor was approached by the local agricultural fair committee to do something spectacular at the upcoming county fair. William agreed but knew he had to protect the reputation of his family, so he decided to pick a stage name for his first public appearance. The newspapers at the time were filled with reports of a dashing Italian war hero and politician whose exotic-sounding name appealed to William—Signor Farini.

On October 1, 1859, the new Signor Farini made his grand debut before a huge crowd, walking a ragged 150-metre rope strung between two buildings, four storeys high, with the

The Great Farini, crossing the Niagara River at Niagara Falls.

Ganaraska River flowing below. Over 8,000 people (twice the population of the town) were entertained by Farini's feats of daring. He walked the high rope blindfolded, doing headstands, leg hangs and somersaults. Farini also performed a strongman act, impressing the audience with an informative medical lecture on anatomy and the benefits of weightlifting.

About a week later, around the time of William's final medical exam, his father returned from England and heard about his son's exploits. Their reunion was so explosive that William left the following day and despite passing his exams, never did practise medicine. He was now the Great Farini, circus performer.

Farini performed high wire acts from southern Ontario to the American Midwest. In 1860 he challenged the famous

The Great Farini, circus impresario.

French daredevil Blondin to the performance of a lifetime. Blondin the Magnificent had stunned audiences the previous year with his amazing high wire act, across the Niagara Gorge. With just ten months' professional experience, Farini challenged Blondin to a high wire duel over the Falls. Blondin ignored him but the Great Farini was as stubborn as he was daring. Eventually Blondin agreed to the challenge.

The competition between the two men soon escalated and grew more and more outrageous. Blondin carried a stove as he walked the rope over the Falls, cooking an omelette when he got to the centre. Farini went one better. Dressed as a woman for comic effect, he took a washing machine out with him and proceeded to do his laundry. Farini followed this act by walking across the tightrope—his whole body inside a sack—and nearly killed himself.

Farini had been remarkably lucky to escape unharmed but in December of 1862 a terrible tragedy took the life of his young wife, acrobat Mary Osborne. Mary had become part of a standard Farini high wire act in which she rode on her husband's back while he performed on the high wire. While performing high above a bullring in Havana, Cuba, Mary turned to wave at the crowd and lost her balance. Farini dropped with her, gripping the rope with his leg as he tried desperately to hold on to the hem of her dress, but the material tore and Mary plunged headfirst into the seats. She died five days later. Farini was devastated and went into seclusion for several months.

Like any true showman, however, Farini knew the show must go on and soon returned to the act. After a couple of years with Barnum Brothers Circus in New York, the Great Farini once again laughed in the face of death. On August 11, 1864, the New York Times reported his craziest stunt of all—a walk through the rapids along the brink of Niagara Falls—on a pair of stilts. Farini managed to get partway across when one of the stilts got stuck in a crevice. Within arm's length of plunging over the American Falls, he somehow managed to survive by pulling himself to safety.

Over the next few years the Great Farini dazzled audiences in Europe and Asia while making London his home. His performances now featured an eight-year-old trapeze artist whom Farini had adopted and called El Nino, "the son." Flying high above the crowds in London's famous Royal Alhambra Palace, Farini and El Nino became overnight sensations, but before long El Nino stopped appearing in the act. Farini was turning 30 and realized he, like El Nino, needed a break from the constant danger of his performances. He and El Nino moved to France where they disappeared from public view.

Eight years later the Great Farini reappeared with a lovely teenage girl named Lulu, the Eighth Wonder of the World. Lulu was an amazing gymnast who made her first appearance in 1870 at the Imperatrice Theatre in Paris. Audiences held their breath as she sprang over 9 metres into the air from the stage onto a trapeze. The Lulu Leap was an immediate sensation and the pair was soon travelling all over Europe. While performing in Dublin in 1876 Lulu missed the trapeze bar and fell. She was rushed to a hospital where doctors discovered that she was a man—Farini's adopted son El Nino.

The older Farini grew, the more outrageous his career became. In 1877 he terrified audiences with the world's first human cannonball act as he fired a young girl named Zazel out of a canon. In the 1880s he toured with the Greatest Show on Earth, introducing freakish acts like "The World's Most Tattooed Man" and "Krau, the Missing Link."

Eventually Farini sought new, more exotic adventures. Along with "Lulu" (now a Connecticut photographer) he explored the Kalahari Desert in Africa. In 1866 Farini published a book about their explorations entitled *Through the Kalahari Desert*, that contained drawings based on Lulu's photographs. In typical Farini fashion the book stirred up considerable controversy by claiming that, somewhere deep in the Kalahari, Farini had discovered the ruins of an ancient civilization. Many doubted the claims he made but there are those who still insist that a lost civilization exists. The debate continues in parts of Africa, where Farini's writings are legendary.

The Great Farini proved to be much more than a successful showman and theatrical agent. He was also an inventor, credited with a variety of clever innovations such as the circus safety net and folding theatre seats. He even gained recognition for his work as a botanist and wrote a book called *How To Grow Begonias*. In 1888 at the age of 50, Farini dazzled a crowd of 65,000 as they watched him jump out of a hot air balloon nearly 1,000 metres above the ground in an invention everybody said would not work—the first modern parachute.

Two years earlier in 1886, Farini had married Anna Muller, the daughter of Kaiser Wilhelm's aide-de-camp. The accomplished young lady was a former pupil of composer Franz Liszt. The couple moved to Toronto around the turn of the century where Farini embarked on several new careers. He turned to painting and sculpting, creating works that were exhibited alongside Canadian masters. Around this time he tinkered with another invention known as Knapp's Roller Boat, reputed to be unsinkable. The idea behind the boat was that passengers would never get seasick in it. The contraption, powered by four steam engines, had a huge steel cylinder with an outer shell that moved with the waves while the inner portion remained stationary. Farini invested $125,000 in the boat which eventually sank, taking his investment with it.

From 1910 to 1920 the couple lived in Germany, returning to Canada to live in Port Hope after the war. The robust 82-year-old Farini continued to paint and was known to exercise daily, often taking lengthy trips around town on his strange-looking bicycle. In 1923 one of Farini's paintings, *Waiting in the Harem*, won an award at the Canadian National Exhibition. He died in Port Hope in 1929 after complications from the flu. The Great Farini was 91.

His former house at 36 North Street has been converted

into the Butternut Inn, one of Port Hope's many bed-and-breakfast establishments. In the centre of town, visitors can stroll through Farini Park. A plaque dedicated in his honour can be found on the Walton Street Bridge over the Ganaraska River. This remarkable man of many talents who taught himself to speak seven languages fluently, dared to be different. In the end, William Leonard Hunt achieved his own unique brand of fame and respectability. Perhaps even his father would have been proud.

The Great Farini, respectable at last.

Part Five

A Question of Identity

Dr. Barry's Secret

ECCENTRIC, TEMPERAMENTAL, ARROGANT AND DIFFI-CULT. These are the words that most often described the peculiar little doctor with the mysterious past.

A young Dr. James Barry.

Everything about Dr. James Miranda Barry was strange, from his undocumented birth and unknown parentage to the astonishing discovery upon his death. His tiny stature, high-pitched voice, effeminate mannerisms and fiery temper made him a social outcast but no one dared question his exceptional medical skill. Famous nurse and humanitarian Florence Nightingale described Dr. Barry as the most hardened creature she had ever met. Others recalled his outrageous—often ridiculous—habits and appearance. He strutted rather than walked. He wore a bright scarlet tunic with fancy epaulettes, an oversized cocked hat with long feathery plumes, and a sword nearly as big as he was. The soles of his high-heeled boots were 8 centimetres thick and wherever he went he was accompanied by his manservant and a little white dog named Psyche.

Dr. Barry cultivated many adversaries in his lifetime mainly because of his quick temper and fierce reactions to teasing and criticism. Many found him so irritating they avoided him as much as possible. When he died the attending staff surgeon, Major McKinnon, could not be bothered performing a final physical examination. It was not until a housekeeper, Sophia Bishop, laid the body out for burial that Dr. Barry's astonishing secret was revealed. The eccentric little red-haired doctor was a woman. Even more shocking, stretch marks on her abdomen indicated that she may have been pregnant at one time. To explain the error and embarrassment, Major McKinnon insisted that Dr. Barry was actually a hermaphrodite but no autopsy was ever performed to confirm the claim. In fact, the Major recorded Dr. Barry as a male on her death certificate. The news of the doctor's sexual identity was so scandalous that British authorities tried to bury the secret along with her, but a story like this could not be hidden for long.

Dr. Barry was born in England around 1799 before the registration of births was made compulsory. Her only proven relative was an artist named James Barry. Researchers believe her mother may have been Ann (Barry) Bulkeley, the artist's sister. General Francisco de Miranda, a Venezuelan exile and close friend of James Barry, may have been the girl's father. The General was known to have one of the largest collections of books in London, including several medical texts that the young girl found fascinating. She yearned to learn more but women of the era were not accepted into universities, let alone schools of medicine.

With a change of name to James Miranda Barry and the guise of a boy, she entered Edinburgh University in Scotland in December of 1809. She was about ten at the time although some reports claim she was a few years older. As incredible as this seems today, in 1809 it was not so unusual for wealthy 12-year-old boys to gain admission to university with the right connections and "correct" payment of fees. Within three years the brilliant young scholar was ready to present her graduation thesis entirely in Latin. She graduated with flying colours.

Now a full-fledged doctor, Barry joined the British Army in the summer of 1813, barely 14 years of age, amid protests from some of the older physicians. Since no physical examination was involved, she was able to keep her true identity a secret. Two years later Dr. Barry was assigned to a colonial post in Cape Town in modern-day South Africa. Her superior medical ability helped her rise quickly through the ranks and she soon became the Physician to the Governor and his family, as well as Assistant Surgeon to the Colonial Inspector.

If anonymity was her plan, Dr. Barry went about it all wrong. Not only did her outrageous outfits attract attention but her arrogance annoyed several of her colleagues who began to question her appearance and her gender. At one point, in order to defend her "manhood," she challenged an offender to a duel over a coarse remark that she overheard.

During her career Dr. Barry received many prestigious honours. In 1822 she was appointed Medical Inspector but quickly made enemies with her uncompromising standards and strict adherence to rules. It was also her task to inspect the prison, a lunatic asylum and a leper colony where she was mortified by the deplorable living conditions she observed.

The outspoken Dr. Barry was a fierce reformer not afraid to challenge the establishment. She presented unpopular new ideas on hygiene and humanity and once again offended the management with her orders and superior attitude. Her expertise, however, went unchallenged. In 1826 while working in Cape Town, she performed the first Caesarean birth in which both mother and child survived.

Over the next thirty years Dr. Barry fought hard to improve hospital conditions wherever she went. In 1836 she was sent to St. Helena, an island off the west coast of Africa, as Principal Medical Officer. St. Helena had a military hospital that was well-equipped, clean and efficient. Conditions in the civilian hospital, however, were atrocious. Dr. Barry tried to convince the military powers in England to send supplies and medicine to treat the women at the civilian hospital where there was a high incidence of venereal disease. Dr. Barry was infuriated with the response from England telling her it was not the duty of the military to interfere in civilian affairs. Ignoring the command to mind her own business, she provided the hospital with assistance. Dr. Barry was arrested and court-martialed for this incident but was acquitted and returned to duty.

When the Crimean War broke out in 1854 and wounded soldiers were sent to Corfu, Dr. Barry was quick to volunteer for service. With her commitment to hygiene and disinfection, she made certain that all uniforms were burned to prevent the spread of disease and infestation. This practice led to a much higher recovery rate for her wounded soldiers than for those treated in other locations.

In 1855 Dr. Barry's visit to the Crimea in the southern Ukraine brought her face to face with Florence Nightingale, another champion in the fight for improving sanitation and hospital conditions. Nightingale found Dr. Barry to be a snob and a tyrant. She was not impressed with the little doctor's superior attitude and was eager to see "him" leave. In a way Florence Nightingale was instrumental in arranging Dr. Barry's Canadian assignment. Nightingale insisted that the Inspector-

General of Hospitals in Canada was needed in England to serve on the Commission for the Improvement of Hospitals, leaving Canada without an Inspector-General. In 1857, nearing 60 and with 44 years of medical experience, Dr. Barry was appointed to fill the prestigious Canadian post.

It was early winter when she arrived in Canada and Dr. Barry immediately became the talk of the town, wearing her flamboyant outfits, strutting like a caricature and giving orders. She attracted a great deal of attention, wrapped in musk ox robes and travelling around Montreal in a magnificent red sleigh complete with silver bells, coachman and footman. As always, she was accompanied by her manservant and Psyche, her little white lapdog. In fact, she named all her dogs Psyche.

Dr. Barry's appointment as Inspector-General of Hospitals for both Upper and Lower Canada was indeed a major promotion for her. As chief military physician in Canada she was given complete authority over hospitals in Montreal, Quebec, Toronto and Kingston. It was the highest appointment possible in Canada's medical profession.

Her first order of business in Canada was to improve the health and welfare of the soldiers. Demanding reforms, she insisted on an improved diet for the troops which included mutton, beef and salt. She criticized the bland meals that the soldiers were fed and demanded that ovens be built for roasting the meat instead of boiling it into a tasteless soup—all this despite the fact that Dr. Barry was herself a devout vegetarian. Next she attacked the water, drainage and sewage disposal systems in the army barracks, claiming that they would lead to sickness and disease. When she learned that married soldiers were forced to sleep in the open barracks with their wives, Dr. Barry insisted on private married quarters in addition to less crowded sleeping quarters for the unmarried troops. While her stay in Canada was relatively short, it produced dramatic changes in the health and welfare of the soldiers' lives.

In May of 1859 she was forced to return to England after contracting a severe case of influenza and developing bronchitis.

Doctors there pronounced her unfit for further duty and placed her on half-pay which greatly reduced her pension. She asked for an extension but was refused, and retired with great resentment and bitterness.

Dr. Barry had expected to be knighted for all her innovations, reforms and 46 years of faithful service as a physician and surgeon, but it was not to be. She saw Florence Nightingale given all the credit for the vast improvement in the diet and living conditions of the soldiers. Unhappy and alone, Dr. Barry died on July 25, 1865, at about 66 years of age.

She was quickly buried but the newspapers got wind of her astonishing secret and printed the shocking revelations. Only then did others come forward to support the housekeeper's discovery, claiming that they knew or had suspected that Dr. Barry was a woman. After the scandal, numerous attempts were made to discredit and undermine her many notable achievements. Her deception was bad enough but the idea of a woman infiltrating the ranks of the British Army, and as a reputable surgeon no less, was unthinkable in the male medical establishment.

This amazing woman, likely the first female doctor in North America, demonstrated outstanding skill and professionalism under the most trying conditions. Dr. James Miranda Barry rose to the highest possible position in the military ranks of medicine. She became the chief military physician in Canada and holds a place of honour in the Federation of Medical Women of Canada. The "beardless lad" who received a medical degree as a child and became famous for her skill and expertise as a surgeon, may have offended many during her lifetime, but to the soldiers and patients whose lives were made better by her reforms, the lady was a hero.

Dr. James Barry with servant and Psyche.

The Real Story
of Grey Owl

WHEN NEWSPAPERS REPORTED THE SUDDEN DEATH OF GREY OWL IN 1938, THE WORLD SUFFERED TWO GREAT LOSSES. People on both sides of the Atlantic bid an emotional farewell to Canada's most famous writer, lecturer and conservationist—a man whose message took him all the way from the backwoods of Canada to Buckingham Palace.

Grey Owl.

Then they learned the unimaginable truth. Their hero was a fraud. The man who called himself Grey Owl and claimed to be the half-Indian son of a Scottish father and Apache mother was really Archibald Stansfeld Belaney, a full-blooded Englishman.

The First Nations people had known for years that Grey Owl was a fake. They had watched in silence as this adopted stranger awkwardly tried to copy their dance steps around their campfires and invented his own peculiar war chants. They watched his antics but said nothing, for here was a man who claimed to be their brother—a man who fought for Aboriginal rights. Who was this man who called himself Grey Owl?

Archibald Belaney was born in 1888 in Hastings, England. His father had a talent for remaining unemployed while "borrowing" countless thousands from his widowed mother. Belaney Senior abandoned his family to marry the teenage sister of his late mistress. Young Archie was raised by his grandmother and his two maiden aunts, Carrie and Ada, with whom he developed a love-hate relationship. The ultra-strict Aunt Ada watched his every move and forced him to use his right hand even though he was clearly left-handed.

Archie had a lonely, miserable childhood. He escaped into a dream world of wide open spaces and no rules. He fantasized about Native peoples living in the wild and at the age of 17 left for Canada to fulfill the dreams of his childhood.

Belaney spent his early years in Canada as a trapper and woodsman in Northern Ontario. In Temagami he met and married the first of his many wives, Angele Egwuna, a young Ojibway maiden. Angele taught Belaney her language and the traditions of her people. After three years of living with the Ojibway, Archie Belaney grew restless. The marriage had produced a daughter named Agnes but following the example set by his own father, Belaney abandoned his wife and child for a life of freedom. Archie became a forest ranger fighting fires in Biscotasing, Ontario. To supplement his income he began writing about his adventures as a trapper and a forest ranger.

Young Archie Belaney, proper English lad in Hastings.

His early articles, published under his real name, appeared in England's *The Hastonian* in 1913.

Around this time he became romantically involved with a young Métis woman, Marie Girard. Archie Belaney began to reinvent himself, working hard to lose his British accent and telling anyone who would listen that his father was a Scot and his mother an Apache. He said he was born in Mexico but was raised as a Plains Indian in Arizona. Life with Marie was pleasant in the beginning but when she became pregnant, Archie abandoned her as well.

By this time World War I was raging in Europe. Archie made his way to Nova Scotia to enlist in the Army. The Englishman-turned-Native went to war wearing a kilt and became a sniper

Grey Owl at home in the woods.

on the front lines. His military career came to a sudden end when he suffered a serious foot injury and was sent to England for surgery. Eventually the fourth toe on his right foot had to be amputated. The injury would bother him for the rest of his life and would confirm his identity after his death.

While recuperating at his aunts' home in England, Archie became reacquainted with an old childhood sweetheart, Florence Holmes. The two were married but when Archie received his military discharge and announced to his bride that they would be moving to the backwoods of Canada, Florence would have none of it. In typical Belaney fashion, Archie threw his wedding band into the harbour and hopped on the first boat back to Canada.

Back home, Archie returned to Angele for four days, just long enough for another child to be conceived before he took off again. He went back to Biscotasing to discover that his Métis spouse, Marie Girard, had borne him a son named Johnny. The boy was being raised by a local woman because Marie had died of tuberculosis. It was not until Johnny was nine years old that he learned Archie was his father. This man who claimed to care so deeply for all living things showed no concern for his own children. Johnny resented his father and referred to him as "Archie Baloney."

Belaney spent the next few years with the Ojibway, perfecting their language and learning their way of life. He dyed his hair black and darkened his skin with henna. He felt at home with the Ojibway and asked them to call him Wa-Sha-Quon-Asin—Grey Owl, the name he adopted to go with his new identity.

At age 36, Grey Owl met a beautiful, well-educated young woman of 19 who would change his life forever. Her Aboriginal name was Anahareo and Archie found himself in love—again. Anahareo's Iroquois father did not approve of the courtship; he had big plans for his daughter's future. Anahareo had received a scholarship to study at the prestigious Loretto Abbey in Toronto, but she was a strong-minded, independent girl and gave up this unique opportunity to live with Grey Owl in his log cabin in the woods.

Anahareo hated the life of a trapper. She had never seen animals being killed and could not bear to witness their pain and suffering. One day she and Grey Owl discovered two tiny beaver kits whose mother had been killed in a trap. Grey Owl was about to shoot the babies when Anahareo stopped him. It would mark a turning point in his life. They took the two beaver kits home and raised them. McGinty and McGinnis became their children. Grey Owl resolved he would never trap another beaver again, a promise he kept even when the couple's money ran out and there was little to eat.

To earn a living, Belaney turned to writing, hopeful that people would enjoy reading about the adventures of McGinty and McGinnis. He sent an article to the editor of *Country Life*, a popular British journal, and received a small publishing contract. Realizing that he could actually make money from his writing, Grey Owl began working on a book, *Men of the Last Frontier*. In the meantime he contacted the Canadian Parks Department suggesting they make a film on his beavers living with people in the wilderness. Audiences loved it. When McGinty and McGinnis unexpectedly returned to the wild, Grey Owl was heartbroken. He focused his attention on the preservation of the beaver population which was being hunted to the brink of extinction, as well as the conservation of Canada's wide open spaces.

Grey Owl's cabin in Saskatchewan's Prince Albert National Park.

The Ministry of the Interior soon moved Grey Owl and Anahareo to Riding Mountain National Park in Manitoba where Grey Owl was made park warden. His primary task was to help increase the beaver population in the area. Water levels in the park lake, however, were too shallow to sustain a new beaver colony. So the government moved them instead to Lake Ajawaan in Prince Albert National Park, Saskatchewan, where there was enough water for the project.

The couple's newly adopted beaver kits, Jellyroll and Rawhide, loved their new surroundings. Grey Owl requested a custom-made log cabin directly on the lakeshore with an opening in the floor. The idea was for the beavers to build their dam partially underneath the house with access to the water, but the furry pair had other plans and created a large mud-covered dam right in the middle of the living room.

A picture of Grey Owl and Jellyroll, disproving the popular notion that adult beavers could not be tamed.

One day Grey Owl brought home a bundle of cedar shingles to repair the roof of the cabin. Jellyroll and Rawhide ate through the metal bands holding the pile together and used the shingles to cover the roof of their own house in the pond. These beaver antics were cleverly filmed by the Parks Service. Grey Owl and his beavers had become media celebrities.

All the while, Grey Owl was writing nonstop, completing other books—*Pilgrims of the Wild* and a children's book, *The Adventures of Sajo and Her Beaver People*. Unfortunately success took its toll on the couple's relationship. Anahareo gave birth to a daughter, Shirley Dawn, for whom Grey Owl had little time or interest. Anahareo found herself neglected and alone as Grey Owl spent all of his time in solitude, consumed with his writing. Eventually she left. Shirley Dawn was raised by close family friends as Anahareo set out to seek new adventures of her own.

Grey Owl's books immediately became popular, especially in Britain. To promote his work the publisher arranged a two-week lecture tour for him. Wearing his buckskins and a full feather headdress and speaking in a low, dramatic voice, Grey Owl became an overnight sensation in England. There was such demand to see and hear what this "real Indian" had to say, Grey Owl's tour was extended to four months. During this time he gave over 200 lectures to an estimated 250,000 eager people. Two members of the audience, however, questioned his identity in silence. Aunt Ada and Aunt Carrie recognized the distinctive Belaney nose but kept the secret.

When Grey Owl returned to Lake Ajawaan he resumed work on his fourth book, *Tales of an Empty Cabin*. Anahareo came back temporarily but soon realized that their relationship was over. She left for good in the fall of 1936 and never saw him again.

Grey Owl was not a man to remain single for long, however. Within a couple of months he married a pretty French-Canadian girl, Yvonne Perrier. He told her about his half-Native background but claimed his English name was McNeil. A

United Church minister married the couple. The names on the record appear as McNeil and Perrier. Grey Owl explained to his bride that he did not think his Aboriginal name would be legal. The truth of the matter was Grey Owl knew that Archibald Belaney was still legally married to his first wife, Angele Egwuna.

Almost immediately Grey Owl set out on another lecture tour of England and the United States, this time accompanied by his new wife. With his dyed hair in braids and dressed in full feathered regalia, he gave a command performance before the Royal Family. This lecture tour proved to be even more successful than his first. In fact the never-ending schedule of performances was so demanding, Yvonne had to be hospitalized for exhaustion when they returned to Canada. Grey Owl, who had been drinking heavily on the trip, told a reporter, "Another month of this lecturing will kill me." At the time he had no idea how prophetic a statement it was.

While Yvonne was recuperating in hospital, an exhausted Grey Owl returned to his cabin on Lake Ajawaan where he soon became ill with a mild case of pneumonia. He called a park ranger and asked to be taken to a nearby hospital where his condition worsened. On April 13, 1938, one month and one day after his fateful prediction to a reporter, Grey Owl slipped into a coma from which he never recovered. He was dead at the age of 49.

The day after his death, the *North Bay Nugget* ran the full story revealing Grey Owl's deception. Actually the *Nugget* had been sitting on the story for a few years. One of their reporters had uncovered the truth about Belaney's past and had written an article exposing the hoax but Ed Bunyan, the editor of the paper, refused to publish it while Grey Owl was still alive. The editor respected the work Grey Owl was doing and would not allow his cause to be undermined by a media scandal.

One week following Belaney's death, a Hastings reporter interviewed his aunts, Carrie and Ada, who talked about their nephew's childhood fascination with the First Nations of North America. The media had a field day covering the juicy details of

Belaney's short life—the drinking, the bigamy, the abandoned children, the fraud and finally, a very public tug-of-war over his will. While Yvonne Perrier "McNeil" was denying all reports that her husband was an Englishman, one of his former wives, Florence from Hastings, said the man who called himself Grey Owl had had a toe amputated in England during the Great War. The funeral home in Prince Albert confirmed that Grey Owl was indeed missing the fourth toe on his right foot. In the ensuing uproar, Grey Owl's entire life's work came under intense public scrutiny and his tremendous contributions as a conservationist and advocate for Aboriginal rights were soon forgotten.

Grey Owl was buried at Lake Ajawaan. A simple cross marks his grave. It reads "A. Belaney" horizontally and "Grey Owl" vertically. Today he is remembered as much for his false identity as he is for his work. He may have acted a part, but he certainly acted it well. Would anyone have listened to what he had to say as Archibald Belaney? No doubt his faults were many but his fight for Native rights and protection of the environment was sincere. Decades later his message still holds true—"You belong to nature; nature does not belong to you."

A Soldier
in Disguise

WHEN SARAH EMMA EDMONDSON WAS BORN IN MAGAGUADAVIC, NEW BRUNSWICK, IN DECEMBER OF 1841, LIBERATED WOMEN WERE FEW AND FAR BETWEEN. Emma, however, was determined not to make the same mistakes as her mother who had married a tyrant at the age of fifteen. Her father, Isaac Edmondson, had hoped for a large family of strong boys to help him work his farm, but instead was blessed with four daughters and a frail, sickly son.

Emma grew up a tomboy—strong, independent and adventurous. As a child she was always in some sort of mischief, riding the wildest horse on the farm, climbing to the top of the highest tree or firing off her father's rifle. In her quiet moments, Emma found an outlet for her imagination in a book that became her inspiration—*Fanny Campbell, the Female Pirate Captain: A Tale of the Revolution.* In this swashbuckling adventure, the heroine disguises herself as a man, takes over a ship and becomes the captain.

Emma Edmonds (she shortened it from Edmondson) was just fifteen when her abusive father tried to force her into an arranged marriage to an older farmer whom Emma found repulsive. With the help of her mother, Emma ran away from home and made her way to nearby Moncton where she landed a job in a millinery shop. Unfortunately a young single girl living on her own was easily noticed and quickly became the topic of conversation. It did not take long for her father to discover where she had gone. Emma knew she would have to resort to drastic measures before he came to get her.

*Sarah Emma Edmonds as Franklin
Thompson, U.S. Civil War soldier.*

Emma disappeared for a while, cropped her hair short, then exchanged her skirts and petticoats for shirts and trousers. She re-emerged as Franklin Thompson, a travelling Bible salesman in Saint John, New Brunswick. In an era where hairstyles and clothing were enough to define a person's gender, Emma's new look passed easily for a young man. According to her autobiography, *Nurse and Spy in the Union Army* (a romanticized version of fact and fiction), she was eager to test the true effectiveness of her disguise back home, and claimed that even her own mother and sisters did not recognize her at first.

"Franklin Thompson" proved to be an excellent salesman. She travelled extensively throughout the northeastern United

States, slowly making her way west. In 1861 Franklin was working near Flint, Michigan, when the U.S. Civil War broke out. Despite her lucrative career in sales, Emma was attracted to the excitement and adventure of the Union cause. In the spring of 1861 she volunteered to serve in the Union Army along with 50,000 other Canadian men. At first Franklin was rejected. The military had a strict height requirement and she was too short. It wasn't long, however, before the Army required more recruits. Passing the physical exam with no more than a firm handshake, Franklin Thompson put on a soldier's uniform and became a male nurse with Company F. The "beardless boy" or "little woman," as Franklin was often called by her comrades, was quickly accepted into the ranks as one of the boys. Although she shared a tent with another recruit, her secret remained well hidden. The soldiers slept in uniform and matters such as personal hygiene were taken care of privately in the bushes. Fooling them all, she fought shoulder to shoulder in the First Battle of Bull Run where she tended to the wounded and witnessed the death of thousands of soldiers ravaged by war and disease.

While stationed in Virginia, Emma/Franklin became personally involved in the anti-slavery movement. In *Nurse and Spy in the Union Army*, she described her feelings of pity and outrage at the deplorable conditions of African Americans. Despite the overwhelming risks involved, Franklin volunteered for a spy mission behind Rebel lines. In order to determine her fitness for this dangerous assignment, she had to undergo another physical examination by a team of Army physicians. This time the firm handshake was replaced by a phrenological exam, a thorough study of the bumps and contours of her head in order to reveal her mental fitness and true character. Franklin passed with no problem and was ready for her assignment—to infiltrate a Confederate fort at Yorktown, Virginia.

Emma disguised herself as a black man by wearing the ragged clothes from a fugitive slave, darkening her skin with silver nitrate and wearing a wig of "real negro wool." One night she sneaked past Rebel soldiers and joined a group of slaves who were assigned to bring food to the Rebels on the lines. To conceal her identity as an agent of the North, she worked long, agonizing hours with the slaves rebuilding Rebel fortifications. For the most part Franklin was accepted, but when the rain and sweat caused the silver nitrate on her face to fade, Emma quickly remarked that she knew it would happen one day, "as her mother was white."

Switching tasks, she then worked undercover carrying buckets of water around the Rebel camp, which allowed her a unique opportunity to check out the post and its fortifications. When she had gathered all the information she needed, Franklin slipped back to the Union lines able to describe the set-up of the fort, the number of troops at the post and the amount of artillery stock.

Her next military disguise was as an Irish peddler woman. No one suspected she was a woman disguised as a man disguised as a woman. While suffering from swamp fever, Emma came upon a dying Rebel lieutenant. He confessed to her that he, too, hated the idea of slavery. Emma took his ring, his watch, a packet of letters and a lock of his hair, and used them to gain access to a Rebel major. Emma won the major's confidence and he asked her to escort twenty-four of his men to recover the body of the dead lieutenant. Emma was provided with a horse which she used at the first available opportunity to escape back to her Union post. En route Emma received her first serious wound when her horse took a bite out of her arm. She managed to make her way to an outdoor field hospital for treatment of the wound and her swamp fever. By some miracle no one discovered her secret. During her recovery Emma continued to serve in the Union army, this time carrying mail for the troops.

Soon after regaining her health Emma returned to spy duty, crossing Rebel lines a total of eleven times. On one of these missions, while disguised as a black female cook, she was able to retrieve some important papers which she picked out of the coat pocket of a Confederate officer. During her escape, however, her mule fell on top of her inflicting a serious leg injury and causing her lungs to hemorrhage. When she arrived once more behind her own lines, Emma asked for nothing more than painkillers. She would not dare go to a hospital for a full medical examination and treatment.

Emma was able to conceal her true identity from Union officials for another two years but according to some biographers, a select few of her comrades were slowly beginning to suspect that "Frank" was not all he pretended to be. These suspicions were written in private journals, however, never voiced aloud. When Emma contracted malaria in Kentucky she realized the game was up. If she went to a military hospital her secret would be revealed. When her request for a leave of absence was denied, Franklin Thompson deserted knowing full well that if caught, she would face a firing squad. Despite her illness, Emma was able to travel as far as Illinois where she checked into a civilian hospital as Emma Edmonds.

Weak and weary from the war, Emma was on the brink of collapse. During her convalescence she began work on an autobiographical novel. Published in 1864, the book became a commercial success selling 175,000 copies, but Emma did not keep her royalties. Both she and her publisher donated hundreds of dollars from *Nurse and Spy in the Union Army* to the Sanitary Christian Commission, the Civil War's equivalent of the Red Cross.

Emma's life took a new and unexpected turn when she met a fellow New Brunswicker. Linus Seelye, a widowed carpenter nine years her senior, and Sarah Emma Edmonds married on April 27, 1867, in Cleveland. The couple moved to Kansas where they managed an orphanage for African-American children. The Seelyes encountered much heartache in their personal life. They lost their own three children and later adopted two. Emma's health, so severely compromised during the Civil War, began to trouble her and the couple knew they did not have the means for costly medical care.

Showing all the pluck and courage that she had displayed time and again during the war, Emma was encouraged to undertake the most daring challenge of her life. With the full support of her equally unconventional husband, Emma applied for a military pension from the U.S. Army. In order to begin the long application process, Sarah Emma Edmonds Seelye had to prove that she actually was Franklin Thompson, a soldier, nurse and spy in the Union army. She had to convince the authorities that her disguise had been necessary for her to carry out her duties. Before her case could be considered, however, the desertion charge had to be forgiven and removed from her record. It was a daunting task, one that required great determination and persistence, not to mention support from former comrades and superior officers. They vouched for her, saying they had no idea Franklin Thompson was a woman. After seven long years the U.S. Senate and House agreed to have the charge of desertion removed from the records of the War Department. Emma was given an honourable discharge and awarded a retroactive pension. In this remarkable precedent-setting case, Emma won the right to a pension for all army nurses regardless of gender. For her next groundbreaking achievement, Emma became the only woman among 350,000 men to be granted membership in the Civil War Veteran's Association and the Grand Army of the Republic.

Living the remainder of her days in Texas, Emma's health deteriorated rapidly, mostly a result of the injuries sustained during the war. Suffering organ failure, paralysis and finally a stroke, she died on September 5, 1898, at the age of 57. Emma was eventually buried in the Washington Military Cemetery in Houston, Texas, possibly the only woman to be buried there. Her tombstone reads: Emma E. Seelye, Army Nurse.

Linus Seelye lived with his family in Fort Scott, Kansas, for a while, then returned to Saint John, New Brunswick, to spend his last few years in his native Canada. He died in 1917.

Fascination with the life of Sarah Emma Edmonds continued into the next century. In 1988 she was inducted into the

U.S. Military Intelligence Hall of Fame and the Michigan Women's Hall of Fame. In 1990 she was admitted to the New Brunswick Hall of Fame. Her legend goes far beyond her disguises, her acts of courage and her social conscience. Sarah Emma Edmonds Seelye will best be remembered as a woman far ahead of her time.

The Strange Case of Susannah Buckler

IT WAS EARLY DECEMBER OF 1735. FOR SEVERAL DAYS A THICK, GREY FOG SHROUDED THE LITTLE HARBOUR OF CHEBOGUE, NEAR YARMOUTH, NOVA SCOTIA. Finally the heavy mist cleared revealing an unexpected ship in the harbour. A few local farmers waited on shore for hours watching for some sign of life, but not a soul could be seen on board. The men decided to investigate.

The ship was the brigantine *Baltimore*, not a name that anyone recognized. As their rowboat touched the vessel, a nauseating stench filled the air. Nervously the men climbed on board where they were confronted by a horrifying scene. Trails of blood and pieces of dry, rotting flesh were everywhere. It was obvious that a violent struggle had taken place yet there were no bodies in sight. The ship had been stripped clean of all its rigging, sails, weapons and cargo. Nothing of any value remained.

The mystery deepened with the discovery that one person, a woman, had survived the slaughter at sea. She had somehow managed to get off the ship and had taken refuge with Charles d'Entremont and his wife, a local Acadian couple. About six months later George Mitchell, a government surveyor, came to the little Acadian village and learned of the incident in the harbour. Mitchell was determined to discover what had taken place aboard the *Baltimore* but the process proved to be complicated and frustrating. The woman's tale left many questions unanswered. By the time Mitchell had found her, months had passed, yet she was apparently still in shock from the traumatic ordeal and became agitated when questioned. Eventually she managed to reveal her name, Mrs. Susannah Buckler, wife of Andrew Buckler, the ship's owner. She offered few details and no one had the heart to question her further for fear of upsetting her again. Meanwhile the ship was left sitting in the harbour.

News of the massacre aboard the *Baltimore* did not come to the attention of the government in the colonial capital of Annapolis Royal until May of 1736. As soon as Governor Lawrence Armstrong learned of the incident, he ordered the woman brought to the capital for a thorough investigation, although Susannah Buckler's mental state was still fragile.

The Governor and His Majesty's Council interviewed Mrs. Buckler at length trying to uncover the truth but they, too, ran into hours of frustration. It was extremely difficult to follow the chain of events leading up to the massacre. Mrs. Buckler's story was confused and her facts were often contradictory.

According to her testimony the *Baltimore* left Dublin, Ireland, on October 7, 1735 and was headed for Boston, Massachusetts. Mrs. Buckler said the vessel put into Chebogue Harbour on the evening of December 16, 1735 to refill its fresh water supply. A few crewmen went ashore for water but did not return. A short while later the ship was attacked by a group of Mi'kmaq who slaughtered the remaining crew and plundered the ship so thoroughly that nothing remained. Mrs. Buckler claimed that she managed to escape the massacre by locking herself in the captain's cabin. When the intruders left, she somehow managed to get off the ship and wandered around the mainland in a daze until she came upon the home of Mr. and Mrs. d'Entremont.

Governor Armstrong and his Council accepted most of Mrs. Buckler's story but many of their questions could not be answered without raising new suspicions. When asked what happened to the bodies of her husband, the captain and the crew, Mrs. Buckler surprised everyone by suddenly offering a conflicting version of the story. She claimed that without a fresh water supply the crew became so weak and sick that they began to die one by one. Before long, corpses began piling up on deck. Her husband, Andrew Buckler, transported the bodies to shore in order to bury them. Finally Andrew Buckler died too.

The Council pressed further. How was it that none of the locals noticed such activity going on within the harbour? If Andrew Buckler went ashore, why did he not return with a fresh water supply? With everyone around her dying of thirst, how was it that only she was able to survive?

Mrs. Buckler continued telling her tale. A few days after her husband's death, several Mi'kmaq came aboard the vessel and seized all the weapons and brandy they could find. She testified that they soon became intoxicated, stripped the ship of all its valuables and forced her to go with them. For several days she lived among the Mi'kmaq, until they finally dropped her off at an Acadian village where she met Monsieur d'Entremont.

Governor Armstrong was an impatient man with a reputation for having a violent, uncontrollable temper. He had once become frustrated with a fellow officer and broken a large glass decanter over the man's head. Although the Governor knew there was more to the story than Mrs. Buckler was telling, he managed to control himself, much to the surprise of the Council. He placed Mrs. Buckler under "open arrest," insisting that she remain in Annapolis Royal until he could verify the details of her testimony.

An extensive correspondence began between Governor Armstrong and Thomas Corker, the ship's agent in Dublin, Governor St. Ovide of Louisbourg, Governor Belcher of Massachusetts, the Duke of Newcastle (the Secretary of State), the d'Entremonts and the Mi'kmaq Chief. The *Baltimore* was brought to Annapolis Royal for investigation.

It was some time before Governor Armstrong's letters were answered. In the meantime sympathy for the poor woman grew in Annapolis Royal. The Governor himself was touched by Susannah Buckler's plight and appeared to accept her story, unleashing his fury at the Mi'kmaq for their role in the incident.

Governor St. Ovide of Louisbourg read the report of the *Baltimore* massacre with interest, surprised that Governor Armstrong was so quick to accept such a questionable account. In the meantime Susannah Buckler lived in comfort, lacking nothing, though officially she was still under "open arrest." At long last Governor Armstrong received some enlightening reports from several of his sources regarding the status of the ship. Slowly, piece by piece, the *Baltimore* mystery began to unravel. True, the ship's owner was Andrew Buckler but a letter from the real Mrs. Buckler made it clear that she had not accompanied her husband on the transatlantic voyage. The letter had arrived from Barbados where Mrs. Buckler and her infant son were awaiting Mr. Buckler's return. The woman who claimed to be Mrs. Susannah Buckler was obviously an imposter and a liar.

The Governor discovered that the *Baltimore* was in fact a convict ship bound for the colonies with over 60 prisoners, only one of whom was a woman. From Chebogue came some startling information. Sixty-six missing indenture certificates had been located. In the 1700s it was common practice for English and Irish authorities to get rid of convicts, debtors and other undesirables by shipping them to the colonies with such papers. Many were forced into indentured servitude, slave labour or army service when they arrived. The woman who called herself Susannah Buckler was one of those convicts.

While at sea, the prisoners somehow broke free of their chains and slaughtered Captain Buckler and the crew, dropping their bodies overboard. Then they went on a murderous rampage, turning on each other until only a few of them were left. Apparently the cause of the riot was "Mrs. Buckler" herself. When the *Baltimore* put into Chebogue Harbour, the surviving convicts were able to escape in the fog. The woman managed to survive the massacre on board by locking herself in the captain's cabin—one of the few true statements from her entire testimony.

Governor Armstrong was infuriated and humiliated at being duped by the false Susannah Buckler. He ordered the imposter brought back before the Council, but it was too late. Weeks before, he had supplied the attractive young woman with money and three influential letters of introduction, one to an acquaintance in Boston, one to the Governor of Massachusetts allowing her to obtain whatever she needed, and the last to a friend in London, directing him to give her a substantial sum of money upon her arrival in England. The clever "Mrs. Buckler" showed her appreciation by offering the *Baltimore* as security for the repayment of the loan. With the generous help of the unwitting Governor, she was able to make her way to Boston and returned to her native Ireland where she vanished.

It was never fully determined who was responsible for the bloodbath aboard the *Baltimore*. Nor was it known who the woman was or what terrible crimes she had committed in Ireland that the authorities would care so little for her safety aboard an all-male convict ship.

As for the *Baltimore*, the real Mrs. Buckler never claimed it. For seven years the "Death Ship," as it came to be known, sat in the harbour until the Governor ordered it to be towed out to sea and burned, taking its terrible secrets with it to the bottom of the ocean.

Whose Coffin
Is It Anyway?

HOW DO TALL TALES GET STARTED? ARE THEY THE PRODUCT OF FABRICATIONS, EXAGGERATIONS OR A VIVID IMAGINATION? NOT ALWAYS. Over the years local stories get passed down from one generation to the next, embellished in the telling and retelling like a message delivered from one player to another in a game of "broken telephone." Details often become altered and confused so that the final version may be quite different from the original.

Sundial memorial erected by friends of Charles Flockton, in Fortune Bay, PEI.

This particular tale was so bizarre that it managed to capture the interest of none other than Robert Leroy Ripley.

A 1927 cartoon sketch in *Ripley's Believe It Or Not* depicted a coffin washed up on a beach with a caption stating, "Charles Coghlan Comes Home!" The article cited specific details of actor Charles Coghlan's coffin on its homebound journey to his favourite summer home in Fortune Bay, Prince Edward Island. It went on to say that the coffin, which was buried in Galveston, Texas, was washed away in a great flood and swept out to sea. The Gulf Stream then carried it on a 3,200 kilometre ocean voyage all the way back to Coghlan's birthplace on the coast of Prince Edward Island.

Actor Charles Coghlan.

It was evident that there were errors in the Ripley account, beginning with the information in the caption. Charles Coghlan was born in Paris, France, and not somewhere in P.E.I. as Ripley had indicated. How did such an incredible story ever get started? Perhaps it had something to do with Coghlan himself. Details of the flamboyant actor's life were just as sensational as the facts surrounding his death.

Charles Francis Coghlan was born in 1841 to English and Irish parents. He was educated as a lawyer but chose instead to become an actor and playwright. He first gained fame on the London stage in the 1860s before coming to America where he was very well received. Before long, Coghlan was considered one of the most highly acclaimed actors of the century. He ranked in fame with stage greats Rose Coghlan (his sister), Lily Langtry and Sir Johnston Forbes-Robertson. In those days Coghlan spent his summers at his adopted home in Fortune Bay. The community was a popular actor's colony. Charming, quaint and peaceful, Fortune Bay provided the perfect retreat for Coghlan's artistic imagination. It was here he wrote several plays that later became successful stage productions.

The tall, handsome actor, known for his charisma and devil-may-care attitude, gained considerable notoriety in 1893 when he married Kuehne Beveridge, granddaughter of the former governor of Illinois. Miss Beveridge, age 19, was a beautiful young actress appearing on the same stage as Coghlan. There was one minor problem, however. At the time, Coghlan already had a wife and a 21-year-old daughter named Gertrude. The public was outraged. Unable to endure such open disapproval by her adoring fans, Miss Beveridge returned to the protection of her grandfather. Meanwhile the first Mrs. Coghlan somehow found it in her heart to forgive her wandering husband and agreed to take him back. Together with their daughter, the couple sought refuge in the peace and quiet of their beloved Prince Edward Island home.

Six years later in 1899 while appearing on stage in Galveston, Texas, Charles Coghlan became ill with an acute case of gastritis. He died unexpectedly on November 27, at the age of 56. On hearing the news of her brother's sudden death, Rose Coghlan sent a telegram to Charles's widow. It appeared in the *Charlottetown Daily Patriot* on December 2, 1899:

Montreal, Que., Nov. 27
Mrs. Charles Coghlan, Galveston:

My heart bleeds for you over poor Charlie's death. My deepest love and sympathies. What will you do with remains? His last words to me as you heard, expressed a wish to be cremated. Do you want to bring him to New York for funeral and cremation? What do you wish? Wire me at once, care Windsor Hotel. Grandma is ill and news must be kept from her.
Lovingly,
Rose

Charles Coghlan's final wish to be cremated was ignored. Instead he was buried in a seaside cemetery in Galveston, Texas. The following year a violent hurricane destroyed the Gulf coast of Texas. When the floods finally subsided, Galveston lay in ruins, much of the shoreline completely washed away. The cemetery was gone forever, swept out to sea like everything else, its contents carried to destinations unknown.

According to legend, a few years later a couple of fishermen standing on the shore of Fortune Bay, P.E.I., spotted a long, rectangular object bobbing up and down on the horizon. They watched as it floated toward the beach, riding the incoming tide. The fishermen towed it ashore, surprised to discover that it was a coffin. Scraping away the thick layer of seaweed and barnacles, they uncovered a silver plate bearing the inscription "Charles Francis Coghlan." The fishermen recognized the name immediately and wasted no time carrying the coffin off to the nearest churchyard cemetery for a proper burial. It was this fantastic tale that captured the imagination of Ripley. Charles Coghlan's daughter Gertrude, however, claimed that after several thousand dollars and years of searching, the body of her famous father was never found.

As if this story were not unusual enough, there is yet another twist to the tale. Some people believe that the coffin belonged to someone else. There used to be another actor who also spent his summers in Fortune Bay—an American named Charles Flockton. In 1894 Flockton purchased Abell's Cape at Fortune Bay and brought his Comedy Company to the island. By coincidence, he even lived in the old house once inhabited by Charles Coghlan. Flockton was so fond of his island home that he wanted his remains buried there when he died.

Actor Charles Flockton.

After his death in 1904, Flockton was cremated, according to his wishes. His ashes were supposedly brought back to Prince Edward Island and placed under a monument near his old home. The monument was erected in his honour by his good friends Mrs. Leslie Carter and David Belasco, a leading New York producer with several smash hits on Broadway. Perched atop this monument is a sundial. An inscription on it reads: "In memory of a faithful friend and loyal servant. The creeping shadow marks another hour of absence. Leslie Carter, David Belasco."

It was this unusual message that initiated a great deal of speculation regarding the fate of Charles Flockton's remains. People argued, if Flockton's ashes were truly brought back to his Prince Edward Island home, what was meant by "another hour of absence"? Skeptics wondered if his ashes were missing. Before long, inquiring minds wanted to know what had actually happened to the remains of Charles Flockton.

Rumours began circulating that sounded very similar to Coghlan's incredible story. In one version, Flockton died during a performance in San Francisco and his distraught daughter buried him in a local seaside cemetery. In 1906 when a devastating earthquake hit San Francisco, the seaside cemetery containing the supposed coffin of Charles Flockton collapsed into the ocean. By some miracle his coffin, carried by strong ocean currents, made its way all around the world to return to Fortune Bay, fulfilling Flockton's wish to be buried there after all.

At this point it is easy to see how the details could have been confused. Over the years the two tales have been told and retold so often that many of the facts have become entwined. Now it remains a mystery that time has made impossible to unravel. So whose coffin was it that floated in from the sea? Was it Coghlan's or Flockton's . . . or perhaps neither?

Part Six

Strange and Mysterious

Gone Without A Trace

THE MYSTERIOUS DISAPPEARANCE OF AMBROSE SMALL HAD ALL THE MAKINGS OF A TABLOID SCANDAL—FAME, WEALTH, CORRUPTION, ADULTERY AND A CLIFF-HANGER ENDING THAT KEPT THE NEWSPAPERS AND POLICE GUESSING FOR YEARS.

Ambrose Small, missing millionaire.

The lead player in this real-life drama was a high profile show business entrepreneur, a millionaire theatre magnate with a golden touch and a lot of enemies.

On December 1, 1919, shortly before his 53rd birthday, Ambrose J. Small scored the biggest financial coup of his career. Amby, as he was known, negotiated a cool $1.7 million deal for the sale of his theatre chain to Trans-Canada Theatres Limited. On December 2 he received $1 million on account with the balance to be paid out over a period of five years. That same day, while his wife Theresa was depositing the million dollar cheque in the Dominion Bank, Amby was out ordering a Cadillac, a fur coat and jewellery for her. Later that afternoon Small met with his lawyer, E.F. Flock, at the Grand Opera House in Toronto to finalize details of the deal. Small invited Flock home for dinner but it was getting late and Flock was anxious to head back to his home in London, Ontario. Flock turned down the invitation and the two men parted company. Ambrose Small left the Grand at 5:30 p.m. and was never heard from again.

In a way Small's mysterious disappearance was typical of him. He led a "shady" life devoted solely to the acquisition of money. Small had the reputation of being a big-time gambler but in fact he never took a chance on anything that was not "fixed" in advance. He also had a mean streak and his greatest satisfaction came from playing malicious tricks on his colleagues—especially if his schemes cost them money, ruined their reputations or destroyed their chances for employment. Amby was not the type of man to take "no" for an answer, and anyone who dared turn down one of his business proposals became an instant target. There was no shortage of people who openly wished him harm.

Despite his ruthlessness, Ambrose Small did have a certain charisma that drew people to him—especially women. He was a short man with piercing blue eyes, an enormous walrus moustache and a magnetic charm that chorus girls found irresistible. In 1902 he married Theresa Kormann, his stepmother's younger sister and the youngest child of the wealthy Kormann Brewing Company family. The couple took up residence in a 16-room mansion in Toronto's exclusive Rosedale district.

With the exception of money, Theresa and Ambrose had very little in common. Unlike her unscrupulous husband, Theresa was a worldly, accomplished musician and an extremely religious woman. In the basement of the Small's Rosedale mansion was a secluded shrine with an altar where Theresa was known to spend many hours kneeling in silent prayer. As for Ambrose, it was a poorly kept secret that while Mrs. Small was on vacation he built a hidden chamber in the Grand Opera House to entertain his budding young starlets. Amby's private room was furnished with a bar, a large luxurious bed and an imposing nude painting on the wall.

Theresa was aware of her husband's numerous affairs but said nothing as long as his flings were kept secret and did not jeopardize her social standing. A few weeks before Small vanished, Theresa discovered an explicit love letter addressed to Ambrose Small from his mistress, Clara Smith. Fearing a scandal, Theresa did not report her husband's disappearance to the police. It was not the first time that Small had slipped away unannounced for a few days with no explanation to his wife or anyone else. When questioned weeks later by the police, Mrs. Small simply replied, "I believe my Amby is in the hands of a designing woman somewhere and will come back." Unfortunately, by the time a concerned friend finally notified the authorities, the millionaire's trail had gone cold.

Ambrose Small was born to hard-working parents in Bradford, Ontario, in 1866. The family moved to Toronto in 1875 where his father, Daniel Small, became the saloon keeper at the Grand Hotel. Daniel was able to get Amby an entry-level job at the Grand Opera House which was right across the road from the hotel. In 1880 Daniel Small became a part owner of the Grand Hotel in which brewing millionaire Ignatius Kormann also had an interest. Ambrose Small's mother died in

1888 and three years later his widowed father married Kormann's older daughter.

By 1889 young Ambrose had risen to the position of treasurer at the Grand Opera House but his sharp tongue and fiery temper eventually got him into trouble with the Grand's manager, Oliver Sheppard. Small decided to move to the Toronto Opera House nearby. Before long the ambitious young man had worked his way up to the position of manager, learning everything he could about the entertainment business. By 1892 Small had managed to acquire enough money (thanks to the racetracks in town) to hold the mortgage on the Toronto Opera House. In 1906 Small was elected president of the prestigious Canadian Theatrical Managers' Association and developed a circuit of 34 theatres across the country. In his day Ambrose Small was one of the best-known personalities in Canada.

By marrying his stepmother's sister, Small gained access to the Kormann fortune, and Theresa's inheritance helped him purchase the Grand Opera House. Small's first order of business was to fire his old adversary, manager Oliver Sheppard, which he did with great satisfaction.

By 1919 Small sensed a decline in the theatre business. Production costs were mounting and the number of theatrical tours coming to town was dwindling. The $1.7 million deal with Trans-Canada Theatres could not have come at a better time. Unfortunately Ambrose Small never lived to enjoy his success—or so it is believed.

The sloppy police investigation into his mysterious disappearance eventually focused on Small's secretary and booking manager of fifteen years, John Doughty. The sale of the theatres to Trans-Canada included a stipulation that John Doughty would be retained with a salary increase and moved to a new office in Montreal. The police tried to interrogate Doughty but they soon learned that he, too, was missing. Doughty had reported for work in Montreal on the 3rd of December as planned but returned to Toronto a couple of weeks later to visit his sisters. He was expected back in Montreal by the 29th of the month but never showed up. The mystery deepened with the discovery that on December 2, the day Ambrose Small disappeared, Doughty went to the Dominion Bank and removed $100,000 in negotiable bonds from Small's safety deposit box.

Speculation ran wild. John Doughty was now the prime suspect but the chief investigator on the case was relying solely on information from psychics and clairvoyants. Based on their intuition, the investigator ordered the Rosedale Ravine dug up in search of Ambrose Small's missing body.

Meanwhile a former janitor of the Grand Opera House told police investigators that he had witnessed a heated argument between Doughty and Small that nearly came to blows. Doughty despised Small and swore he would kill him and take the theatre money. The police eventually found Doughty working in a sawmill under an alias in Portland, Oregon. Doughty was charged with the theft of the missing bonds but he insisted he knew nothing about the whereabouts of Ambrose Small. Under interrogation he confessed that the bonds could be found in a brown paper bag at the home of his sisters. He claimed that he had kept them there for safekeeping, that the bonds were not stolen and that they had been given to him by Ambrose Small as a reward for his years of faithful service.

Doughty's story was never taken seriously, as everyone who knew Small understood he was not the sort of man to give away anything—especially to an employee. Doughty was convicted of stealing the bonds from Small's safety deposit box but the charges of kidnapping and murder were dropped.

Theresa Small, in the meantime, had become a recluse, and was afraid to leave her home. She refused to speak to anyone except immediate family members or priests and nuns from her church. She began to spend more and more time alone before the altar in her basement shrine. Rosedale suddenly became a tourist site as people came to gawk, hoping to catch a glimpse of Theresa. News reporters hounded her mercilessly, pounding on her doors and windows for an interview. The Small home on Glen Road even became one of the stops on a tour of famous homes in Toronto. Visitors came from all over the continent to see the house where the missing millionaire had lived.

Theresa, too, made headlines when she decided to bequeath the entire Small fortune to the Catholic Church, which enraged the predominantly Protestant population of Toronto. When Ambrose Small's sisters protested that their brother had changed his will in 1918 to include them, the newspapers again were filled with gossip about the rich and famous.

One of the theories that captured the public's imagination was that Theresa Small was not as pure and pious as she had led everyone to believe. Some claimed that she had a lover in London, Ontario, and the two of them planned her husband's murder. The night watchman at the Grand Opera House in London told police that he had spoken to Small on the night of December 2. A caretaker claimed that he smelled fumes coming from the furnace and pointed an accusing finger at Theresa and her lover for killing Small and then incinerating him to hide the evidence. The London police searched the Grand Opera House from top to bottom, practically taking the theatre apart in the process, but nothing was ever found.

Theresa Small died on October 14, 1933 after a long illness. She was buried in a simple grave with no headstone, afraid that curiosity seekers would never let her rest in peace.

Years of litigation eventually resulted in a settlement of Ambrose Small's estate. After all the legal bills were paid, Small's original $2 million in assets could barely pay the creditors.

The mystery of Ambrose Small has never been solved. Legend has it that his ghost still makes the odd appearance at his beloved Grand Theatre in London, Ontario, and has never missed an opening night.

Falsely Accused

HIGH ON A HILL IN LUNENBURG, NOVA SCOTIA, ARE TWO FAMOUS LANDMARKS—THE LUNENBURG ACADEMY, NOW AN ELEMENTARY SCHOOL, AND BESIDE IT, HILLCREST CEMETERY. A walk through the cemetery reads like a page from a local history book. Tombstones recall names and events from a long and colourful past.

A most unusual gravesite with a tragic story to tell.

Among the tombstones, one stands alone, a tall granite shaft bearing a most unusual inscription:

ERECTED BY
SYMPATHIZING FRIENDS
IN MEMORY OF
SOPHIA L.
DAUGHTER OF JOSEPH AND LAVINIA
MCLAUGHLIN
WHO DIED SUDDENLY
SEPTEMBER 19, 1879

———

FALSELY ACCUSED
SHE DIED OF A
BROKEN HEART.
BEFORE HER DEATH SHE
REFERRED HER ACCUSER
TO THE FOLLOWING
TEXTS OF SCRIPTURE
EXODUS XX, 16
MATTHEW V, 10 11,12

Who would have thought that Sophia L. McLaughlin's simple life would have the makings of such high drama? She came from a family of hard-working labourers. Her father, Joseph, and grandfather, Benjamin, built small sailing vessels —dories and whalers mainly. Sophia's mother Lavinia was a stern, serious woman with little time for sentiment or tenderness. She had six daughters—Sophia, the eldest, followed by Elizabeth, Eldora, Ella May, Luthia and Althoea. The family rented a small cottage on Pelham Street just down the road from Sophia's grandparents. They were ordinary folk living ordinary lives.

Like most early settlements, Lunenburg suffered its share of hardships and misfortune. The McLaughlins were no exception. On October 12, 1878, Ella May, age six, died of scarlet fever. Sophia was 13 at the time. Two days after Ella May's passing, three-year-old Althoea died. Sophia was crushed. As the eldest she had often been a "second mother" to the girls, and their sudden deaths were a devastating loss.

Sophia became depressed and quickly lost interest in school. She took a position as an apprentice to a well-known dressmaker named Anne Trask. Mrs. Trask had two children, Charles (about the same age as Sophia) and Nellie (two years younger). Mrs. Trask was a native of Nova Scotia; her children were listed as being American. There is no record of a husband.

Sophia proved to be a capable dressmaker's apprentice and seemed content in her new occupation. She was an honest, dependable worker. In her few moments of spare time, Sophia could be found quietly reading her Bible. Mrs. Trask knew she could trust Sophia to take care of the shop while she ran errands around town.

It was on one of these occasions that Sophia witnessed an event that changed her life forever. Mrs. Trask had gone out for the day leaving Sophia on her own. At some point, however, Sophia realized that she was not alone in the shop. A short while later Mrs. Trask returned and discovered that ten dollars (a considerable sum of money in 1879) was missing from her drawer.

Mrs. Trask was furious and instantly turned her rage upon Sophia, accusing her of theft. Sophia tried desperately to defend herself but Mrs. Trask refused to listen. She was fired from her job and sent home.

Sophia turned to her family for comfort and support but found none there. Lavinia was humiliated by the scandal. Her only concern was that her daughter had disgraced the family. Joseph McLaughlin was well-liked and respected by the community. His business was built upon a reputation of reliability and trust. Lavinia feared that Sophia's actions would reflect badly on them all.

Sophia had nowhere to turn. She trudged up the steep roads to the cemetery where she threw herself on her sisters' graves and wept openly. All the while, Mrs. Trask spread the word around town, threatening to have Sophia arrested. Sophia returned to her sisters' gravesite time and again, crying bitterly, swearing her innocence in the stillness of the cemetery.

Sophia now found herself totally abandoned. Her family was humiliated. Friends avoided her. Even her own mother had turned against her. Finally Mrs. Trask informed the McLaughlins that a warrant had been issued for Sophia's arrest.

Sophia became ill and insisted that these false accusations were killing her. Lavinia paid little attention and sent Sophia to her room. In the morning the sheriff would be coming to take her to jail.

In the loneliness of her room, a sudden change took place in Sophia. Perhaps she found strength in the belief that she would soon be with her beloved little sisters. Sophia assured her mother that before long her innocence would be known to everyone, and for the first time in days she claimed to "feel easy now and happy." Confined to her room, Sophia wrote a long letter to Mrs. Trask.

Sometime later a visitor dropped by unexpectedly. She took one look at Sophia and knew instantly that something was terribly wrong. Lavinia protested but eventually gave in and agreed to call a physician. By the time the doctor arrived, it was too late. On Friday, September 19, 1879, Sophia McLaughlin passed away.

News of her death spread quickly through the town, and with it the speculation of how such a tragedy had come to pass. Was it suicide? Was it murder? Could she have been poisoned? The attending physician called for an immediate inquest to put these rumours to rest. A coroner's jury made up of several well-respected members of the community met in the afternoon to try to make sense of the mysterious death. After some deliberation the jury reached a unanimous decision. The verdict was documented for the record: "Death occurred as a result of paralysis of the heart brought on by extreme agitation caused by peculiar circumstances." Sophia McLaughlin, age 14 years, 6 months, became known as the girl who died of a broken heart. She was buried on September 22, 1879. The family, too poor to afford anything more, marked her grave with a simple wooden cross.

Shortly after Sophia's death, Charles Trask confessed to the theft. The money supposedly was found under his mattress.

Sophia's tragic story was published in the local newspaper along with the letter she had written in her final tormented hours. Mrs. Trask's and Charles's names were omitted from the original publication.

Dear Mrs. Trask

It is now just half past nine o'clock, and I am sitting down to write you a few lines, and doing it to remind you of what you have accused me, so innocent, for you blamed me for stealing your money but there is One above knows that I did not take it. Nothing would tempt me to do so. Mrs. Trask, you will cause my death, and it is a fearful thing. It can't be concealed forever; it will come out some day, and then what will your feelings be? You know that if you have any fear of God that it is awful to be blamed if you are innocent. I was writing this letter when you was down. I was never brought in a scrap like this in my life. You will never have me to blame again. I am nearly gone; my hand trembles so that I can scarcely write. There will be many a long hour that you will think of this, if you have any heart at all. I would not take a false oath, but I did not take your money. You know it is a fearful thing to lie. What it is ever in this world, it is in the next.

Mrs. Trask, take the Bible and turn to the XX Chap. Of Exodus and tell Charles to read the 16th verse of it for my sake. You also take Matthew, Chaps. V, VI and VII; read them; see if there are not verses that will answer this. For example take the 1st verse of the VII, and the 10th, 11th and 12th verses of the V Chapters.

Mrs. Trask, you know that when I am gone they can say what they like; but of what they say I am innocent of, and I am not afraid to fear death. I know a secret but I ain't going to say anything about it, but I won't say that I will never tell you. I can't write anymore.

From your friend,
Sophie L. McLaughlin

When you hear that song, "My grave, my grave, keep green," think of me! Mrs. Trask, you have to make it out the best way you can. Think how this will disgrace my father, mother, and sisters and all belonging to me, but you brought it on. Good bye for ever!

No one knows I wrote you this letter. You can tell my people about it when I am gone.

The town mourned the terrible tragedy in which they had all played a part by turning their backs on an innocent girl. Something had to be to done to honour the memory of Sophia. Shortly after the article appeared in the *Progress*, the citizens of Lunenburg contributed to a special fund to erect a proper headstone for Sophia's grave.

Sophia's gravestone stood in Hillcrest Cemetery marking her final resting place for over a century. Many visitors were puzzled by the unusual inscription, but several in the community knew the sad story and were troubled by the injustice that caused this young, innocent girl to die in vain.

In 1986 the Bluenose General Radio Service (GRS) Society of Lunenburg decided to get involved in a special community project. Sophia's tombstone had deteriorated over time. The GRS Society put forth a motion to have Sophia's gravesite restored and made easier to locate within the grounds. The town of Lunenburg, eager to right a wrong after so many years, rose to the occasion.

The gravestone was sandblasted. A local ironworker created a decorative iron fence and railing, along with two mounted plaques describing the events leading to Sophia's tragic death. The cemetery commission allowed a fence to be erected around the monument even though the commission's bylaws prohibited fencing within the cemetery grounds. On September 19, 1986, 107 years after Sophia's death, a dedication service was held at the cemetery.

Sophie McLaughlin's gravesite. A town rights a wrong.

Three years later, on September 19, 1989, the GRS Society published a little blue booklet entitled "SOPHIA." The material was researched, written and financed by the Bluenose GRS Society. It was presented to the Lunenburg Board of Trade for distribution to the visitors of the town.

Over the years, many have asked why Sophia kept the thief's identity a secret. Did Charles threaten her? Unlikely.

Was she afraid that no one would believe it was Mrs. Trask's own son who took the money? Possibly. Or was it something much more powerful that caused her to suffer in silence? Was Sophia secretly in love with Charles and willing to protect him at all costs? Why else would she allow herself to be so falsely accused?

The inscription on Sophia's tombstone refers to the letter she wrote to Mrs. Trask just before her death. The verses she quoted from the Bible are not on the stone but they appear on one of the wrought iron plaques at the foot of her grave.

> *Exodus XX, 16*: Thou shalt not bear false witness
> against thy neighbour.
> *Matthew V, 10*: Blessed are they which are
> persecuted for righteousness' sake: for theirs is
> the kingdom of Heaven.
> *Matthew V, 11*: Blessed are ye, when men shall
> revile you, and persecute you, and shall say all
> manner of evil against you falsely, for my sake.
> *Matthew V, 12*: Rejoice, and be exceeding glad: for
> great is your reward in Heaven: for so
> persecuted they the prophets which were
> before you.
> *Matthew VII, 1*: Judge not, that ye be not judged.

The Dark Side
of the Island

CENTRE ISLAND, WARD'S ISLAND AND HANLAN'S POINT, THE MOST WELL-KNOWN OF THE TORONTO ISLANDS, ARE A SHORT 20-MINUTE FERRY RIDE FROM CANADA'S LARGEST CITY. At one time the islands were part of a peninsula connected to the mainland by a long, sandy spit of land. In 1858 a violent storm washed away this natural bridge, separating the peninsula from the mainland.

Each island has its own unique charm. They have been host to a number of newsworthy events, such as the first home run ever hit by Babe Ruth as a professional baseball player. Away from the hustle and bustle of the city, the islands offer beaches, parkland, an amusement centre, a petting zoo and biking and jogging trails. Yet in the midst of this recreational retreat stands a reminder of a dark and mysterious past.

The island lighthouse was built in 1808 at Gibraltar Point at the tip of what is today Centre Island, near Hanlan's Point. Strategically located, the lighthouse played an important role in the defence of the muddy town of York (Toronto).

The first lighthouse keeper was J.P. Rademuller, a man with a questionable history. He was a schoolteacher from Germany who moved to England where he found employment tutoring children. Rademuller soon left England amid accusations of impropriety and decided to make a new start overseas. He took the job of lighthouse keeper in York. During the War of 1812 Rademuller acted as a lookout for the British, watching for signs of American ships approaching on Lake Ontario.

*The Toronto Island Lighthouse, the city's oldest
standing brick structure.*

Rademuller occupied a small cabin beside the lighthouse.
He lived a solitary, lonely life, often entertaining himself and a
group of British soldiers stationed nearby with a keg of moonshine. The War of 1812 had ended but the British felt the need
to maintain a presence in the area. They were still nervous
about the possibility of another American attack. The soldiers
sent to occupy the blockhouse at Gibraltar Point often sought
a drink to break the boredom of their assignment. Liquor was
strictly forbidden at the barracks but they knew they could
count on old Rademuller and his bootlegging operation near
the base.

On January 2, 1815, Rademuller mysteriously disappeared. What happened to him has never been fully determined, but the chilling details that later unfolded became legendary.

It was bitterly cold that night when three British soldiers came to the lighthouse in search of Rademuller, presumably to buy some moonshine. After a few drinks the soldiers became loud and aggressive. They demanded another round but Rademuller was afraid to sell them any more. A vicious fight broke out and in a drunken rage they clubbed Rademuller to death.

Two of the soldiers were eventually arrested for the murder of J.P. Rademuller. Witnesses came forth to testify that they had seen three soldiers attacking the victim, but only two of the soldiers could be positively identified. The soldiers were released, however, because Rademuller's body could not be produced as evidence of his murder. The public was outraged. Local newspapers condemned the soldiers' conduct and demanded justice, but legally there was no case since no one knew what had become of the body.

It wasn't until 1852, 37 years later, that a grim discovery by the third lighthouse keeper, James Durnan, and his nephew, George, shed some light on the mystery. While digging in their garden not far from the lighthouse, they accidentally uncovered part of a human skeleton. According to some accounts, Durnan unearthed an old jawbone so fragile it crumbled into dust in his hands. When Durnan and his nephew discovered these skeletal remains, the full story of Rademuller's murder finally unfolded.

Apparently, after Rademuller had been murdered, the soldiers realized the enormity of their crime and knew they had to conceal the evidence. They decapitated and then dismembered Rademuller's battered body, scattering and burying the various body parts to the west of the lighthouse.

Island folklore has it that after the murder, the beacon in the lighthouse continued to shine though no one was there to light the lamp. Many theories arose to explain the strange phenomenon, the most bizarre being that the eerie light was actually the ghost of Rademuller searching for his lost head. And, there were even those who swore that on dark, stormy nights they could hear the moans and groans of old Rademuller in the howling of the wind.

Today the lighthouse remains in its original location maintained as an historic site. It is the oldest brick structure still standing in Toronto and the oldest lighthouse in the province. On the stone exterior, a plaque was erected officially recognizing the lighthouse's reputation as a haunted building.

The Lake Light

The plaque on the lighthouse describing the building's colourful history. It reads:

THIS LIGHTHOUSE, ONE OF THE EARLIEST ON THE GREAT LAKES, WAS COMPLETED IN 1808 AS AN HEXAGONAL TOWER 52 FEET [16 METRES] HIGH, TOPPED BY A WOODEN CAGE WITH A FIXED WHALE-OIL LANTERN. IN 1832 IT WAS RAISED TO 82 FEET [25 METRES] AND LATER EQUIPPED WITH A REVOLVING LIGHT. THE MYSTERIOUS DISAPPEARANCE OF ITS FIRST KEEPER, J.P. RADEMULLER, IN 1815, AND THE SUBSEQUENT DISCOVERY NEARBY OF PART OF A HUMAN SKELETON, ENHANCED ITS REPUTATION AS A HAUNTED BUILDING.

The Phantom Train
Disaster

GUS DAY WAS ENJOYING HIS RETIREMENT. HIS CAREER
WITH THE CANADIAN PACIFIC RAILWAY IN MEDICINE HAT,
ALBERTA, HAD BEEN A PRODUCTIVE ONE DESPITE THE
TERRIBLE MEMORY OF ONE TRAIN WRECK THAT
HAUNTED HIM EVERY DAY OF HIS LIFE. In his retirement,
Gus kept himself busy by working as a stationary engineer at
the Union Club in Victoria, B.C., recalling old railroad days
with his friends and reading *The Locomotive Engineer*, a weekly
newspaper for railway personnel.

*Collision between Engine #702 and Passenger Train #17, which
killed seven people, including Robert Twohey and James Nicholson.*

One evening Day read a headline that made his heart race. Splashed across the pages of the newspaper was a story describing a "phantom train" that had recently been sighted in Colorado. Gus shuddered as he read the news article. All the memories and the pain of that terrible morning came racing back. For many years he had tried to put the chilling details out of his mind, but now he was forced to remember them all over again.

It was June of 1908 and stoker Gus Day was working for the CPR on a train from Medicine Hat to Dunmore. His job was to keep the fires going in the locomotive's boiler. The engineer was Robert Twohey, a seasoned veteran of the railway with whom Day had worked on several runs. Their task that unforgettable night was to couple with the Spokane Flyer and take it west to Lethbridge before heading into the Crowsnest Pass, a railway clearing high atop the Rockies. Day and Twohey were about 3 kilometres out of Medicine Hat, rounding a blind curve on a hill, when an oncoming train appeared out of nowhere. The two trains were travelling on the same track, heading toward one another at full speed. The approaching train whistled its warning but disaster seemed inevitable, a collision just seconds away.

Gus Day recalled the sight of the oncoming train's headlight as being about the size of a wagon wheel. He shouted to Twohey in horror and got ready to jump off the train. Engineer Twohey was about to grab the brake valve when his hand stopped in mid-air. The approaching train whistled again, then suddenly swerved and rushed past them. Day and Twohey stood frozen as they watched coach after coach pass by. The crew inside the train waved a customary greeting as if nothing out of the ordinary had taken place, even though both trains had been travelling in opposite directions on the same track.

Day and Twohey were speechless as they exchanged bewildered glances. They began to wonder if they had been seeing things. Embarrassed by what the other might think, neither of them would discuss the strange experience. They continued on

Searching the wreckage for survivors.

to Dunmore as originally scheduled, picked up the Spokane Flyer and completed their run in silence.

A couple of weeks later Gus Day and Robert Twohey happened to meet on a street in Medicine Hat. Finally one of them broke the silence and they began to talk about their close encounter on that single railroad track. What a relief it must have been for Twohey and Day to know that they had both experienced the same eerie feeling and witnessed the same strange phenomenon.

For Twohey, however, it was much more than just an eerie feeling. He confessed to Day that a few weeks before seeing the phantom train, he had visited a fortune teller in town who warned him that his time was near. She claimed he would be dead within a month. At first he dismissed the prophecy as nonsense—after all, he was in perfect health and at the height of his career—but Twohey was visibly shaken. The thought of an accident had never occurred to him before. Now he could think of little else. To be on the safe side, he decided to take some time off and stayed away from the rail yards for a while. His co-worker, Gus Day, remained on the job as before.

For a few weeks life continued without incident. Gus Day was beginning to think that perhaps the events of the past would fade like a bad dream. But it was not to be. One evening shift Day was assigned to the same engine on the same run as before. James Nicholson replaced Robert Twohey as engineer.

Once again the train left the station in Medicine Hat and headed toward Dunmore. They rounded the same curve in the tracks and were approaching the same spot on the hill when Nicholson gasped in horror. An oncoming train was rushing furiously toward them at top speed, its whistle blowing sharply and its headlight shining brightly in the darkness. Nicholson and Day braced themselves for disaster when all of a sudden the phantom train sped past them on phantom tracks. Just as before, coach after coach passed them by, the crew members in the phantom train waving their customary greetings. A stunned Gus Day and James Nicholson could do nothing but stare at each other in disbelief. They continued on their way to Dunmore in silence as the phantom train disappeared once more into the blackness of the night.

Gus Day continued to work on the trains for the remainder of the month but his nerves were shot. On the morning of Wednesday, July 8, 1908, he was assigned to yard duty. He was relieved to stay off the trains for a while. Taking his place as stoker was Harry Thompson; James Nicholson stayed on as the engineer. Their engine, #702, pulled out of the Medicine Hat station shortly after eight o'clock in the morning, heading toward Dunmore to pick up the Spokane Flyer and take it further east to Swift Current, Saskatchewan.

As before, they headed into the hills around the curve in the tracks. James Nicholson stirred uneasily as they approached the same spot where the phantom train had been seen. Suddenly another train appeared around the curve speeding straight for them, but this time it was daylight and the train was real. Passenger Train #17 was coming in from Lethbridge heading for Medicine Hat. Amid frantic whistles and deafening screeches, the inevitable happened. The two trains collided in a huge cloud of steam and smoke. When the dust cleared, a scene of death and destruction littered the tracks. James Nicholson's outbound train was crushed, its boiler head torn off. The two trains had ripped each other apart, the passenger train's engine telescoping through the mail and baggage cars, and right into the first tourist car. All three cars had toppled off the tracks and were lying in the ditch.

Just moments before the fateful accident, stoker Harry Thompson had spotted a farmer standing at the top of the hill who was waving his arms frantically in the air. From his position on the hill, the farmer could see both the outbound and inbound trains rushing toward each other. Thompson assumed the farmer was merely waving at them as they passed. All of a sudden Thompson realized what was happening. He managed to jump off the train a split second before the disastrous collision. Unfortunately James Nicholson was not as lucky. He pulled the brake in a frantic last minute attempt to save his train but it was too late. Nicholson was killed instantly in the terrifying wreck.

The death toll on the approaching train was far worse. Four people were killed on impact—two passengers, the stoker and the baggage handler. A number of others sustained injuries but they managed to survive the crash. Two were critically injured. One was Philip Millett, the conductor. The other was the engineer, a man who had taken some time off work to overcome his fear and thought it was now finally safe to return. This man was Robert Twohey. Engineer Twohey was found lying under some bushes. He was barely conscious and in tremendous pain.

Millett and Twohey were rushed to Medicine Hat. By the time they arrived at the hospital, Twohey had collapsed and was in shock. Millett's skull was hopelessly fractured. He died in hospital at 4:20 that afternoon. In the meantime, Twohey's condition worsened. Suffering from massive internal bleeding, he would not recover.

Gus Day was working in the rail yard in Medicine Hat when he learned that his friend Robert Twohey had died in a coma following a train disaster.

An inquest was held to determine the cause of the accident. The verdict pointed to two men. Station operator H.B. Ritchie had failed to notify the engineer that incoming Train #17 had not yet arrived. Engineer James Nicholson had failed to check the train register to make sure the track was clear before pulling out of the station and heading east.

Gus Day mourned the loss of his friends and colleagues. He cared little about the results of the inquest. He was not interested in who was to blame. All he could think about was that phantom train rushing toward him on the same track. Twice he had witnessed the strange encounter—once with Robert Twohey and once with James Nicholson. Now both of them were gone and he alone was left with the chilling memory. But perhaps someone else knew as well—a fortune teller in Medicine Hat who had warned Twohey that he would be dead within a month's time.

The Medicine Hat Train Station.

The Loss
of the *Fairy Queen*

CHARLOTTETOWN, PRINCE EDWARD ISLAND, HAS HAD ITS SHARE OF TRAGEDIES AT SEA BUT ONE IN PARTICULAR WAS SO HAUNTING IT STANDS OUT FROM ALL THE REST. On the morning of October 7, 1853, Captain Cross woke early and headed into town. In the distance, the silence of the morning was broken by the distinct sound of a bell coming from the direction of the harbour. Eight times it tolled. A strange sensation overcame the captain as he quickened his pace. The bell rang again. This time the sound seemed to come not from the harbour but from the heart of town. Captain Cross couldn't imagine who would be awake so early in the morning. The bell rang again, but not like before. This time it was a continuous dull ringing like the haunting echo of a fog bell. Captain Cross turned toward the wharf to see if a ship was in trouble.

The only thing the captain saw was a steamer, the *Fairy Queen*, with a few rough-looking crewmen working to keep it tied to the dock. Once again the bell tolled. Captain Cross knew something was wrong as he was drawn along Kent Street toward the centre of town.

The captain made his way to the street corner and gazed nervously in the direction of the sound. It was definitely coming from the old Presbyterian church, the Kirk of Saint James. He approached the church staring at the belfry, expecting to find a logical answer, when out of the corner of his eye he noticed three women at the entrance to the church. They stood in bare feet, dressed in simple white robes, unaware of his presence. His attention was drawn to the tower as the bell began to toll again. Captain Cross caught a glimpse of a fourth woman in white up in the belfry. He wondered if she was the one who had been ringing the bell all morning. The captain looked back at the entrance, but the women had disappeared and the church door was slowly closing.

The captain ran to the door and tried the latch but it was locked. Suddenly a hand tapped him on the shoulder. He spun around to discover a familiar face. It was Davy Nicholson, the church sexton, who had also heard the mysterious tolling of the bell and had come to investigate. Together the two men tried the door but it was bolted shut. They ran around the church hoping to find an unlocked door somewhere but the building was

The original Kirk of St. James,
Charlottetown, Prince Edward Island.

sealed. Peeking through a tiny window, they saw the figure of a woman in white slowly climbing the stairway to the bell tower. The two men stared as she disappeared from view.

Captain Cross stood guard at the church door while Nicholson raced to fetch the Reverend Snodgrass and the church keys. The captain could hear the sound of footsteps and faint voices inside the church but he could not get into the building. Finally Nicholson returned with Reverend Snodgrass. They unlocked the door and entered but found the church empty. The captain and the sexton started up the stairs to the belfry, sending the Reverend to wait outside.

The hatch to the belfry was extremely heavy and Nicholson struggled awkwardly to lift it. He could not understand how those delicate ladies had managed it on their own. When Nicholson and Cross entered the belfry, the bell was still vibrating. They looked all around the tower, but as difficult as it was to believe, there was absolutely no trace of the women anywhere.

The two men made their way down the stairs and stepped outside to explain the strange sequence of events to Reverend Snodgrass, who firmly dismissed their entire story as pure nonsense. The Reverend was a very persuasive man. In fact he had such a powerful effect on the sexton that Davy Nicholson began to doubt what he had seen just moments before. Captain Cross continued to put forth a strong argument but it was useless. The Reverend ridiculed the idea of the tolling bell and the women in white, though he never questioned the captain's sincerity. Captain Cross was known to be a reliable, highly-respected citizen of excellent character. He was a man of reason and logic with little patience for superstition, but Reverend Snodgrass still insisted that the captain must have been mistaken.

The Reverend did call on several people in the neighbour-hood, however, and discovered that other trustworthy residents had also heard the bell at the same time. Later that afternoon, in the cold, choppy waters of Northumberland Strait, a bizarre chain of events unfolded—events so startling that they would cause the Reverend to reconsider Captain Cross's story.

At six o'clock that eerie morning of Friday, October 7, 1853, the *Fairy Queen* had been scheduled to leave but Captain William R. Bulyea delayed departure because of high winds. The waters of Northumberland Strait were still churning from a late night storm. Captain Bulyea knew better than to test his wretched steamship in this kind of weather. Thirteen unsuspecting passengers had arrived at the dock and were greeted by the sight of the freshly painted, polished vessel. Little did they know that beneath the bright exterior was a death trap not fit for any kind of travel, let alone a dangerous journey across turbulent waters.

Captain Bulyea had been promised a cash payment for a quick mail delivery to the mainland, and gave little thought to the safety of his passengers or the twelve ruffians he had hired as crewmen. The wind subsided around noon, making the waters in the harbour appear deceptively calm, but Bulyea knew the Strait would still be treacherous.

As the steamer left the shelter of Charlottetown Harbour, the passengers and crew realized they were in danger. The *Fairy Queen* was tossed about by the angry seas. The rotting old hull creaked and groaned. Suddenly the ship sprang a leak. Then another. The tiller rope broke, making the ship impossible to steer. Bulyea barked orders to have the anchor released over the bow in a desperate attempt to keep the vessel steady and pointing into the wind. The waves kept battering the hull and breaking over the deck. The crew and passengers were given buckets to bail out the water but it was hopeless. By five o'clock the rising water had put the boiler fires out.

Captain Bulyea ordered the lifeboats to be lowered as the ship was slowly sinking. The two lifeboats could hold a total of thirty-four people, certainly enough room to accommodate everyone on board. At around eleven o'clock that night Captain Bulyea, the mate and eight crewmen climbed aboard the two lifeboats. For reasons unknown, instead of loading the rest of the people into the boats, they slashed the ropes, setting themselves free. Amid the screams and cries, the captain and his chosen crew left the rest to struggle alone aboard the doomed ship. Panic swept the deck as those left behind watched their only real hope of survival drift away.

In desperation they began ripping boards off the deck, lashing them together with remaining pieces of rope to build a makeshift raft. Then without warning, the ship broke in two. Nine of the remaining people managed to cling to the raft. They were able to hang on for eight long hours in the cold, stormy sea until they reached land. The other seven people, four women and three men, plunged helplessly into the raging waters and drowned.

Captain Bulyea and his crew were picked up the next day. They were later tried, convicted and imprisoned for acts of gross negligence and cowardice.

IN MEMORY OF
N. COLIN MacKENZIE. M. D.
ARMY MEDICAL STAFF, A NATIVE OF
ROSSHIRE SCOTLAND.
WHO PERISHED IN THE WRECK OF THE STEAMER,
FAIRY QUEEN, NEAR PICTOU ISLAND OCT. 7. 1853:
LANDING ON THIS ISLAND AN ENTIRE STRANGER.
HE BECAME DURING AN OFFICIAL STAY
OF TWO YEARS THE INTIMATE FRIEND OF
MANY AND GAINED THE ESTEEM OF ALL.
THIS TABLET
RECORDS THE SORROW OCCASIONED BY
HIS DEATH, AND ESPECIALLY THE LOSS
SUSTAINED BY THE POOR
TO WHOSE SUFFERINGS HE EVER ATTENDED
WITH PROMTITUDE AND BENEFICENCE.
AN: ŒB: XXVI:
HIC SEDEBAT

Plaque inside new Kirk of St. James honouring one of the parishioners who perished on the Fairy Queen.

Within a few days news of the *Fairy Queen* reached the shores of Charlottetown. Captain Cross and Davy Nicholson recalled at once the persistent tolling of the church bell in the early hours of that fateful day. They remembered the strange chain of events that led them to the Kirk of St. James and the sight of the four mysterious women in white. They remembered, too, the look of utter disbelief on Reverend Snodgrass's face when they tried to convince him of what they had witnessed. Of the seven who drowned, four were women. The other three were members of the church. Was it merely a coincidence or a message of impending doom? Seven people were lost along with the *Fairy Queen*. The bell had tolled eight times altogether. Reverend Snodgrass, deeply saddened and bewildered, could say nothing.

Bibliography

Abbott, Elizabeth, ed., *Chronicle of Canada.* Montreal: Chronicle
 Publications, 1990.
Ashman, Dee Cherrie, *Carved in Stone: The Legend of Willie.*
 Wiarton, ON: Dee Cherrie Ashman, 1996.
Barnes, Theodore, *Fine Canoe: Prairie Steamboat Day Revisited.*
 Toronto: McClelland & Stewart Ltd., 1977.
Basque, Garnet, *Canadian Treasure Trove,* Vol. 1. Vancouver:
 Garnet Publishing Co., 1973.
Basque, Garnet, ed., *Lost Bonanzas of Western Canada.* Langley,
 BC: Sunfire Publications Ltd., 1990.
Basque, Garnet, ed, *Lost Bonanzas of Western Canada,* Vol. II.
 Langley. BC: Sunfire Publications Ltd., 1994.
Belliveau, John Edward, *Running Far In: Story of Shediac.* Windsor,
 NS: Lancelot Press, 1970.
Berton, Pierre, *My Country—The Remarkable Past.* Toronto:
 McClelland & Stewart Ltd., 1976.
Big Beaver Historical Society, *Happy Valley Happenings.* Regina:
 W.A. Print Works Ltd., 1983.
Billinghurst, Jane, *The Many Faces of Archie Belaney: Grey Owl.*
 New York: Kodansha Int., 1999.
Borrett, William Coates, *Tales Retold Under the Old Town Clock.*
 Toronto: Ryerson Press, 1957.
Boulton, Marsha, *Just a Minute.* Toronto: Little, Brown & Co., 1994.
Boulton, Marsha, *Just a Minute More.* Toronto: McArthur, 1999.
Boulton, Marsha, *Just Another Minute.* Toronto: Little, Brown & Co.,
 1997.
Bremner, Benjamin, *An Island Scrapbook: Historical and Traditional.*
 Charlottetown: Irwin Printing Co. Ltd., 1932.
Brewster, Hugh, *Sinking Sensation,* in *Toronto Life,* May 1997.
Brown, Ron. *Fifty Unusual Things To See in Ontario.* Erin, ON: The
 Boston Mills Press, 1989.
Burles, Gordon, *Bill Peyto,* in *Alberta History,* Vol. 24 #1, Winter
 1976. Historical Society of Alberta.
Callbeck, Lorne C., *My Island, My People.* Charlottetown: Prince
 Edward Island Heritage Foundation, 1979.
Canadian Army Journal, 1955.

Canadian Geographic, November/December, 1993.

Canadian Veterinary Journal, November, 1993.

Carlisle, Norman, *Cockney Lord of the Beaver Lands,* in *True Magazine,* Canadian Edition.

Cash, Gwen, *Off The Record.* Langley, BC: Stagecoach, 1977.

Chard, Donald F., *The Last Voyage of the Baltimore,* in *Nova Scotia Historical Review,* Vol. 7, No. 2, 1987.

Charlesworth, Hector, *More Candid Chronicles.* Toronto: The MacMillan Co. of Canada Ltd., 1928.

Charlottetown *Daily Patriot,* November 29, 1899; December 2, 1899.

Christy, Jim, *Strange Sites: Uncommon Homes and Gardens of the Pacific Northwest.* Madeira Park, BC: Harbour Publishing, 1996.

Colombo, John Robert, *Colombo's Canadian References.* Toronto: Oxford University Press, 1976.

Colombo, John Robert, *Mysterious Canada.* Toronto: Doubleday Canada Ltd., 1988.

Cook, Greg, *A Woman, a Man, a Nurse, and a Spy,* in *The New Brunswick Reader,* September 18, 1999.

Crooker, William S., *Oak Island Gold.* Halifax: Nimbus Publishing Ltd., 1993.

Dannett, Sylvia. *Noble Women of the North.* New York: T. Yoseloff, 1959.

Dannett, Sylvia, *She Rode With the Generals.* New York: Thomas Nelson & Sons, 1960.

Dempsey, Hugh. *The Golden Age of the Canadian Cowboy.* Saskatoon: Fifth House Publishers, 1995.

DesBrisay, Mather Byles, *History of the County of Lunenburg.* Toronto: William Briggs, 1895.

Dictionary of Canadian Biography, Vol. 9. Toronto: University of Toronto Press, 1976

Downhomer, The, May 1983.

Enroute Magazine, September 1981, Vol. 9, #9.

Evans, Millie, *Oak Island, The Unsolved Mystery.* Tantallon, NS: Four East Publications, 1993.

Evans, Millie & Eric Mullen, *Nova Scotia's Oak Island. The World's Greatest Treasure Hunt.* Tantallon, NS: Four East Publications Ltd., 1984.

Ferguson, Bob, *Who's Who in Canadian Sport.* Toronto: Summerhill Press, 1985.

Filey, Mike. *Toronto Sketches.* Toronto: Dundurn Press, 1992.

Furneaux, Rupert, *Buried Treasure.* London: Macdonald Educational Ltd., 1978.

Furneaux, Rupert. *The Money Pit Mystery. The Costliest Treasure Hunt Ever.* Letchworth, Eng.: The Garden City Press, 1972.

Galgay, Frank and McCarthy, Michael. *Shipwrecks of Newfoundland and Labrador,* Vol. 2. St. John's: Creative Publishers, 1990.

Gibson, Sally, *More Than an Island: A History of the Toronto Island.* Toronto: Irwin, 1984.

Globe and Mail, Nov. 25, 1925; Dec. 1, 1926; Dec. 7, 1926; March 4, 1932; March 23, 1932; March 24, 1932; Nov. 17, 1936.

Gould, Ed, *All Hell For a Basement – Medicine Hat 1883-1983.* City of Medicine Hat, 1981.

Hacker, Carlotta. *The Book of Canadians.* Edmonton: Hurtig Publishers, 1983.

Harkness, John Graham, *Stormont, Dundas and Glengarry, A History.* Ottawa: Montreal Press Ltd., 1946.

Hart, E.J., *Ain't It Hell: Bill Peyto's "Mountain Journal".* Banff, AB: EJH Literary Enterprises, 1995.

Hawkes, John, *The Story of Saskatchewan and its People.* Regina: S.J.Clarke Publishing Co., 1924.

Heritage House, *Outlaws and Lawmen of Western Canada,* Volume 3. Surrey, BC: Heritage House Publishing Company Ltd., 1987.

Higgins, David Williams, *Tales of a Pioneer Journalist.* Surrey, BC: Heritage House Publishing Co., 1996.

Hustak, Alan, *Titanic: The Canadian Story.* Montreal, Vehicule Press, 1998.

Hutchinson, Geoff. *Grey Owl: The Incredible Story of Archie Belaney.* Brede, England: Geoff Hutchinson, 1985.

Jenish, D'Arcy, *The Airborne Exploits of Father Goose,* in *MacLean's Magazine,* May 27, 1996.

Kalman, Harold, *Exploring Vancouver 2.* Vancouver, U. of British Columbia Press, 1978.

Kluckner, Michael, *Toronto, The Way It Was.* Toronto: Whitecap Books (Toronto) Ltd., 1988.

Lindsay, F.W. *The Cariboo Story.* Quesnel, BC: F.W. Lindsay, 1958.

Lishman, William, *Father Goose.* Toronto: Little, Brown and Co., 1995.

Lownds, M. Russell, *The Sea, Ships, and Sailors.* Halifax: Petheric Press, 1970.

Ludditt, Fred W. *Barkerville Days.* Vancouver: Mitchell Press, 1969.

Lunenburg GRS Society, *"Sophia",* Lunenburg, NS: Lunenburg GRS Society, 1989.

Lunenburg *Progress-Enterprise,* September 23, 1879, February 22, 1967, September, 1986.

Luxton, Norman; Luxton, Eleanor, ed., *Tilikum: Luxton's Pacific Crossing.* Sidney, BC: Gray's Publishing Ltd., 1971.

MacEwen, Grant, *Fifty Mighty Men.* Saskatoon: Modern Press, 1958.

MacEwan, Grant, *Mighty Women.* Vancouver: Greystone Books, 1975.

MacKenzie, Michael, *Memories Recalled.* Christmas Island, NS: MacKenzie Books, 1992.

MacKenzie, Michael, *Remember the Time....* Grand Falls, Nfld.: Christmas Island, N.S.: MacKenzie Books, 1981.

Marquis, Greg, *In Armageddon's Shadow.* Montreal: McGill-Queen's University Press, 1998.

McClement, Fred, *The Strange Case of Ambrose Small.* Toronto: McClelland and Stewart Ltd., 1974.

McCrae, Archibald Oswald, *The History of the Province of Alberta.* Edmonton: Western Canada History Co., 1912.

McDonald, R.A.J. and Barman, Jean, editors, *Vancouver Past: Essays in Social History.* Vancouver, U. of British Columbia Press, 1986.

Medicine Hat *News,* July 8, 16, 23, 1908; March 24, 1983.

Moose Jaw *Evening Times*, February 18,1924; April 2, 1925.

Moose Jaw *Times-Herald*, June 19, 1972; August 1, 1981; April 26, 1985; February 17, 1986; May 29, 1987; September 11, 1987; April 23, 1990; August 7, 1993; April 19, 1995; September 6, 1995; March 27, 1996; June 22, 1997; July 8, 1997.

Morrow, Don and Keyes, Mary, *A Concise History of Sport in Canada.* Toronto: Oxford University Press, 1989.

Mullin, L.J., Owens, Eldon, and Meacher, Dick, *Together At Last: Tom Sukanen and His Ship.* Moose Jaw, SK: Ferguson Printing Ltd., 1999.

Musson, James, *Grand Delusions: Henry Hoet and Cobblestone Manor.* Edmonton: Brightest Pebble Publishing Co. Inc., 1995.

New Brunswick Reader, The. September 18, 1999

O'Connor, D'Arcy, *The Money Pit.* New York: Coward, McCann, & Geoghegan, Inc., 1978.

Orkin, Mark M., *The Great Stork Derby.* Don Mills, ON: General Publishing Co., 1981.

Owen Sound *Sun Times,* February 2, 1994; February 3, 1995; May 25, 1995; April 10, 1996; February 3, 1997; February 3, 1999; February 4, 1999.

Panati, Charles, *Extraordinary Endings of Practically Everything and Everybody.* New York: Perennial Library, 1989. New York: Perennial Library, 1989.

People Magazine, October 14, 1996.

Peck, Mary. *The Bitter With the Sweet.* Tantallon, NB: Four East Publications, 1983.

Plaskett, William, *Lunenburg, An Inventory of Historic Buildings.* Lunenburg, NS: Town of Lunenburg, 1984.

Raddall, Thomas H., *Footsteps on Old Floors.* Porters Lake, NS: Pottersfield Press, 1988.

Ray, Isobel, *The Strange Story of Dr. James Barry.* Toronto, Longman's, Green & Co., 1958.

Ramsay, Sterling, *Folklore Prince Edward Island.* Charlottetown, P.E.I.: Square Deal Publications, 1974.

Rendle, J. Edward., *The Phantom Bell Ringers.* in *The Prince Edward Island Magazine*, Vol. 1, no. 10, Dec.1899.

Riley, Dan; Primrose, Tom, and Dempsey, Hugh, *The Lost Lemon Mine.* Calgary, AB: Frontier Publishing Ltd., 1968.

Robertson, John Ross, *Landmarks of Toronto.* Toronto: J. Ross Robertson, 1894.

Robertson, Linda, *Sergeant Bill of the Fifth,* in *Heritage Review,* Spring 1989.

Rose, June, *The Perfect Gentleman.* London: Hutchinson & Company, 1977.

St. John's *Evening Telegram,* November 25, 1991, December 2, 1991.

Sayer, Francis R., *A History of Shediac Cape.* Shediac, NS: F.R. Sayer, 1966.

Scanlon, Kevin, *Father Goose,* in *Equinox Magazine,* March/April, 1990.

Sherwood, Roland H., *Maritime Mysteries: Haunting Tales from Atlantic Canada.* Hantsport, NS: Lancelot Press, 1976.

Sherwood, Roland, *Sagas of the Land and Sea.* Hantsport, NS: Lancelot Press, 1980.

Shilliday, Gregg, editor. *A History of Manitoba, vol.3.* Winnipeg: Great Plains Publications, 1995.

Smith, Barbara, *Ghost Stories of Alberta.* Willowdale, ON: Hounslow Press, 1993.

Smith, Laura, *A Matter of Mystery.* Yarmouth, N.S.: Sentinel Printing, 1993.

Spalding, Jane (project co-ordinator), *The Lost Lemon Mine.* Edmonton: Lone Star Publishing, 1991.

Starkell, Don, *Paddle to the Amazon.* Toronto: McClelland & Stewart, 1987.

Starkell, Don, *Paddle to the Arctic.* Toronto: McClelland & Stewart, 1995.

Stewart, Ron, *The Mystery of the Lost Lemon Mine.* Langley, BC: Sunfire Publications Ltd. 1993.

Stone, Ted, *Alberta History Along the Highway.* Red Deer, AB: Red Deer College Press, 1996.

Stone, Ted, *British Columbia History Along the Highways and Waterways.* Red Deer, AB: Red Deer College Press, 1998.

Students of Toronto Island Public School, *A History of the Toronto Islands.* Toronto: The Coachhouse Press, 1972.

The Loose Moose News, produced by Tourism Moose Jaw.

Toronto *Star,* August 29, 1903; March 31, 1934, December 8, 1973; February 3, 1999.

Townshend, Adele, *Drama at Abells Cape,* in *The Island Magazine,* Spring-Summer 1979

Tunnels of Little Chicago. Articles courtesy of Edward Behr, Nancy Gray, Larry Schaak, and Gina Knelsen Schall.

Vacation Guide, May 1982, May 1983.

Walkem, W. Wymond. *Stories of Early British Columbia.* Vancouver: News-Advertiser,1914.

Wallace, W. Stewart, *Murders and Mysteries.* Toronto: Macmillan Co. of Canada Ltd., 1931.

Watson, Julie V., *Island Beaches.* Tantallon, N.S.: Four East Publications, 1988.

Weber, Bob, *Saskatchewan History Along the Highway*. Red Deer, AB: Red Deer College Press, 1998.

Weekend Magazine, in Winnipeg *Tribune*, July 19, 1958.

Wheelwright, Julie, *Amazons and Military Maids*. London, Eng.: Pandora Press, 1989.

Wilson, Herbert Emmerson, *Canada's False Prophet: The Notorious Brother 12*. Toronto: Simon and Shuster of Canada Ltd., 1967.

Woodcock, George, *Faces From History*. Edmonton: Hurtig Publishers Ltd., 1978.

Woodcock, George, *100 Great Canadians*. Edmonton: Hurtig Publishers, Ltd., 1980.

Yee, Paul, *Saltwater City*. Vancouver, Douglas & McIntyre, 1988.

Credits

The authors thank the following individuals and groups for permission to reproduce images:

Page 3 courtesy of Bill Lishman; pg. 7 courtesy of Bill Lishman; pg. 9 courtesy Bill Lishman, photo by Ted Liss; pg. 10 courtesy Bill Lishman, photo by Ted Liss; pg. 11 courtesy The Glass House, photo by Dorse McTaggart; pg. 13 courtesy The Glass House; pg. 14 courtesy The Glass House; pg. 15 courtesy The Glass House; pg. 18 courtesy Thunder Bay Historical Museum Society 985.34.8; pg. 20 courtesy Thunder Bay Historical Museum Society 905.34.11; pg. 26 photo by Ted Liss; pg. 27 photos by Ted Liss; pg. 29 courtesy Sukanen Ship Pioneer Village and Museum; pg. 33 courtesy Sukanen Ship Pioneer Village and Museum, photo by Ted Liss; pg. 35 courtesy Laurene Shaw Sabey; pg. 38 photo by Ted Liss; pg. 40 photo by Ted Liss; pg. 43 courtesy Toronto Reference Library; pg. 48 photo by Ted Liss; pg. 52 photo by James Masters, Courtesy *The Sun Times,* Owen Sound; pg. 54 City of Vancouver Archives CVA 287.2; pg. 57 City of Vancouver Archives BUP 140.N.90; pg. 58 Glenbow Archives, Calgary, Canada NA.14512.9; pg. 60 Provincial Archives of Alberta OB.3169; pg. 64 photo by Ted Liss; pg. 70 courtesy Moose Jaw Public library Archives; pg. 71 courtesy Moose Jaw Public Library Archives; pg. 72 courtesy Charlotte's Restaurant, photo by Ted Liss; pg. 75 courtesy Moose Jaw Public Library Archives; pg. 78 B.C. Archives C-05791; pg. 87 courtesy Don Starkell; pg. 89 courtesy Jeff Starkell; pg. 92 courtesy Don Starkell; pg. 93 courtesy Don Starkell; pg. 96 courtesy Wayne Mushrow; pg. 98 courtesy Wayne Mushrow; pg. 103 Glenbow Archives, Calgary, Canada NA-1438-1; pg. 104 photo by Ted Liss; pg. 105 photo by Ted Liss; pg. 109 courtesy Eleanor Luxton Historical Foundation/Whyte Museum Box 18; pg. 110 photo by Ted Liss, courtesy Maritime Museum of British Columbia; pg. 112 courtesy Eleanor Luxton Historical Foundation/Whyte Museum Box 14; pg. 116 Nova Scotia Archives and Records Management, Robert

Norwood Collection, Acc, 1987 481; pg. 118 Nova Scotia Archives and Records Management, Robert Norwood Collection, Acc, 1987 481; pg. 120 photo by Ted Liss; pg. 123 photo by Ted Liss; pg. 127 courtesy Mabel MacLean; pg. 128-129 courtesy Mabel MacLean; pg. 134 photos by Ted Liss; pg. 136 Saskatchewan Archives Board, R-A10210-1; pg. 140 courtesy Broadview Museum, Photo by Ted Liss; pg. 146 (top) Public Archives of Canada C-1879; pg. 146 (middle) National Film Board of Canada; pg. 146 (bottom) courtesy Ted Liss, pg. 147 (top) courtesy Ted Liss; pg. 147 (bottom) courtesy Manitoba Archives 71-1937; pg. 149 Toronto Reference Library; pg. 155 City of Toronto Archives SC 608-59; pg. 162 Archives of Ontario AO 843; 164 Archives of Ontario S 17740 Acc 6282 F1073; pg. 165 Archives of Ontario AO 4814 F 1073; pg. 169 Archives of Ontario S 17232 Acc 6282 F 1073; pg. 173 The Wellcome Institute Library, London, L 22266; pg. 179 The Wellcome Institute Library, London, L22267; pg. 180 National Archives of Canada PA-122479; pg. 182 National Archives of Canada PA-147585; pg. 183 Saskatchewan Archives Board R-B2570-2; pg. 185 Saskatchewan Archives Board 68-955-01; pg. 186 Glenbow Archives, Calgary, Canada NA 3680-8; pg. 191 Clarke Historical Library, Central Michigan University 2034; pg. 202 photo by Ted Liss; pg. 203 Toronto Reference Library; pg. 206 courtesy Cora McKenzie; pg. 211 Toronto Reference Library; pg. 217 photo by Ted Liss; pg. 223 photo by Ted Liss; pg. 226 photo by Ted Liss; pg. 228 photo by Ted Liss; pg. 229 Medicine Hat Museum & Art Gallery Archives PC 22.6; pg. 231 Medicine Hat Museum & Art Gallery Archives PC 22.9; pg. 234 photo by Ted Liss; pg. 236 PEI Public Archives and Records Office 2702175; pg. 239 photo by Ted Liss.

Cover images from top left down:
    Clarke Historical Library, Central Michigan University 2034
    Glenbow Archives, Calgary, Canada NA-1438-1
    Courtesy Don Starkell
    Courtesy Mabel MacLean
    Courtesy of Bill Lishman;
    Courtesy Eleanor Luxton Historical Foundation/Whyte
        Museum Box 18.

Index

A

Anahareo, 184-87
  birth of daughter, 187
  meets Grey Owl, 184
Armstrong, Governor Lawrence, 198-201
astrolabes, 97-98

B

Baltimore, 197-201
  massacre, 197, 200
Banff, Alberta, 103-04
Banff National Park, 106
Barkerville, B.C., 130, 135
Barley, Alfred and Annie, 80
Barr, Elinor, 19
Barry, Dr. James Miranda, 173-78
  in Canada, 177
  in Cape Town, 175-76
  Crimean War, 176
  parents, 174-75
  sexual identity, 174, 178
  in St. Helena, 176
Baumgartner, Myrtle, 81-82
Bearspaw, Chief Jacob, 61
Bearspaw, King, 65
Belaney, Archibald Stansfeld see Grey
  Owl
Belasco, David, 207
*Believe It Or Not see Ripley's Believe It Or
  Not*
Bendow, Daniel, 61
Bendow, William, 61, 63
Bennett, Walter, 97
Berglund, Tony, 19
Beveridge, Kuehne, 204
Blackjack, the prospector, 59-61
Blair, Frederick, 120
Blankenship, Dan, 121-22, 123
Blondin the Magnificent, 166
Bluenose General Radio Service Society,
  222, 223
Bowdoin, Henry, 120
Boyd, Mabel, 80, 81
Broadview, Saskatchewan, 137, 139, 140
Brother Twelve, 78-83
  aliases, 79
  Aquarian Foundation, 80, 83
  disappearance and death, 83
  Eleven Masters of Wisdom, 79

  feeding pigeons, 80-81
  The Three Truths, 79
Brouwer, Sam, 49, 50, 51, 53
Brown, David, 11-17
  building house, 14, 16
  collecting bottles, 12-13
  early life, 12, 16
  as funeral director, 12
Brown, Eldon, 16, 17
Brown, Margaret (Molly), 158-60
Buckler, Captain Andrew, 200
Buckler, Susannah, 197-201
  false testimony, 198-99
  deception revealed, 200
Bulyea, Captain William R., 238-39
Bunyan, Ed, 188
Butt, John, 66-69
  paralysis, 68
  as street cleaner, 67
  and tea party, 69
  as thief, 69
  as town crier, 66-67
Butternut Inn, 169

C

Cameron, Alice, 130
Cameron, Cariboo, 127-35
  Cameronton, 132, 135
  in the Cariboo, 130-31, 132, 135
  second marriage, 133
Cameron, Sophia, 127, 129-31
  first burial, 131
  fourth burial, 133
  second burial, 132
  third burial, 133
Cameronton, B.C., 132, 135
Capone, Al, 71
Card, Charles Ora, 36
Cardston, Alberta, 35-36
Carpathia, 159
Carrick, Bill, 6-7
Carter, Leslie, 207
Centennial Trans-Canada Canoe Race,
  88
Champlain astrolabe, 98-99
Chang Toy, 55-57
Charlottetown, P.E.I., 235
Chinese Immigration Act, 71
Chow, Jack, 56

Cobblestone Manor, 36, 37-40
Coghlan, Charles, 203-07
 Ripley's Believe It Or Not, 203-04
 death and burial, 205
 marriage, 204
Coghlan, Gertrude, 205-06
Coghlan, Rose, 204, 205
Comtois, Melina, 150, 151, 152
Connally, Mary, 81-82, 83
convict ships, 200
Cotton, Dr. T.H., 44
Cross, Captain, 235-37, 240
Curwain, Daisy, 137, 139
Curwain, Fred, 137
Cyr, Louis, 148-53
 in the circus, 152
 death, 153
 grandfather, 150
 health problems, 152
 parents, 148
 tour of England, 151
Cyr, Pierre, 150

D
Day, Gus, 229-34
Decarie, Hector, 153
Derby, Mary, 25
Dontianen, 34
Doughty, John, 214-15
Duff, Joseph, 8
Durnan, James, 227

E
Edmonds, Emma, 190-96
 becomes Franklin Thompson, 191
 burial, 195
 desertion, 194
 joins Union Army, 192
 marriage, 194
 military pension, 195
 Nurse and Spy in the Union Army,
  191, 192, 194
 parents, 190
Edmondson, Sarah Emma see Edmonds,
 Emma
Egwuna, Angele, 181, 184
El Nino, 167
Eleven Masters of Wisdom, 79
England, Robert, 80, 82
Entremont, Charles d,' 197

F
Fairy Queen, 235, 238-40
False Prophet, 83
Farini, the Great see Hunt, William
 Leonard
Father Goose, 6
Fighting Fifth, Western Cavalry, 137, 139
Flickinger, Ed and Arlene, 36, 39-40
Flock, E.F., 212
Flockton, Charles, 206-07
Fly Away Home, 4, 8, 9
Fort Douglas, Manitoba, 144-45
Franklin, Sir John, 94
French, Lafayette, 62-65

G
Gaboury, Marie-Anne, 141-45
 children, 142-44, 145
 marriage, 141-42
Gibson, Jane, 21
Girard, Marie, 182, 184
Grand Opera House, 214, 216
Great Stork Derby, 46-47
Grey Owl, 180-89
 Anahareo, 184-87
 Angele Egwuna, 181, 184
 aunts, Carrie and Ada, 181, 187, 188
 books, 185, 187
 children, 184, 187
 deception revealed, 188-89
 Florence Holmes, 183-84
 Marie Girard, 182, 184
 parents, 181
 as park warden, 186
 World War I, 182-83
 Yvonne Perrier, 187-89
Groundhog Day, 49, 50
Groves, Margaret Sophia see Cameron,
 Sophia
Guinness Book of World Records, 88

H
Hannington, William, 24-28
 marriage, 25-26
 monument, 26, 28
 treasure map, 28
Hawkes, Allen G., 73-77
Historic Resources Act, 99
Hitchens, Robert, 157-59
Hoet, Henry, 36-40
 building Cobblestone Manor,
  37-39
Holmes, Florence, 183-84
How to Grow Begonias, 168
Hudson's Bay Company, 144
Hunt, William Leonard, 162-69
 death of wife, 166
 El Nino, 167
 highwire debut, 163-64
 How to Grow Begonias, 168
 inventions, 168
 Knapp's Roller Boat, 168
 Niagara Falls challenge, 166
 second marriage, 168
 Through the Kalahari Desert, 167-68

I
imprinting, 6-7
Isle aux Morts, 97

J
Jason, Victoria, 93-94
Johnson, Walter, 73-77

K
Kee, Sam see Sam Kee
Knapp's Roller Boat, 168
Kormann, Ignatius, 213-14
Kormann, Theresa see Small, Theresa

L
Lagimodière, Jean-Baptiste, 141-45

Lagimodière, Laprairie, 143-44
Lagimodière, Reine, 142-43
Lee, Edward, 98
Lemon, the prospector, 59-62
L'Heureux, Jean, 61-62
Lightoller, Charles, 157-58, 159
Lishman, Bill, 3-10
    artistic career, 5-6
    Autohenge, 6
    Father Goose, 6
    Fly Away Home, 4, 8, 9
    house, 8-10
    marriage, 4
    Moonship on Earth, 5
    The Last Buffalo, 6
    training geese, 6-8
    Transcending the Traffic, 6
Lishman, Paula, 4, 6
Lorenz, Konrad, 6-7
Lost Lemon Mine, 64, 65
Lunenburg, Nova Scotia, 217, 222
Luxton, Eleanor, 114-15
Luxton, Norman, 109-15
    in Banff, 114-15
    Crag and Canyon, 114
    as journalist, 110
    in South Sea islands, 111-12
    and Stoney First Nations, 114
    Tilikum, 111-13

M
Madame Zee *see* Skottowe, Mabel
McDougall, Georgina, 115
McDougall, John, 61-62
McGinnis, Daniel, 117-19
McKenzie, Mac, 50
McLaughlin, Lavinia, 218, 219, 220
McLaughlin, Sophia, 218-24
    death, 220
    family, 218, 219
    letter, 221-22
McOuat, Jimmy, 19-23
    building the Castle, 22
    curse, 21-22
    death, 22
Michaud, David, 150
Millar, Charles, 43-47
    Great Stork Derby, 46-47
    will, 45-46
Millett, Philip, 233
Miranda, General Francisco de, 174-75
Mitchell, George, 197
Money Pit, 116-23
    Oak Island Association, 119-20
    Oak Island Treasure Company, 120
    Onslow Company, 119
    Restall family, 121
    Triton Alliance, 121-22
    Truro Company, 119
Moose Jaw, Saskatchewan, 71-77
    Brunswick Hotel, 76
    Cecil Hotel, 76-77
    police force, 74-76
Mullen, Moon, 34
Muller, Anna, 168
Mushrow Astrolabes I and II, 102
Mushrow, Lloyd, 97

Mushrow, Wayne, 96-102
    extortion charge, 100, 102
    first astrolabe, 97-101
    Mushrow Astrolabes I and II, 102
    second astrolabe, 101-02

N
Nicholson, Davy, 236-37, 240
Nicholson, James, 232-33
Nightingale, Florence, 174, 176, 178
Nolan, Fred, 122
Nurse and Spy in the Union Army, 191, 192, 194

O
Oak Island Association, 119-20
Oak Island, Nova Scotia, 116-17
Oak Island Treasure Company, 120
Onslow Company, 119
Orinoco River, 91
Osborne, Mary, 166

P
Paddle to the Amazon, 92
Paddle to the Arctic, 95
Peguis, Chief, 144-45
Perrier, Yvonne, 187-89
Peuchen, Major Arthur, 154-61
    Standard Chemical Company, 156
    Titanic stigma, 159-60
    World War I, 160
Peyto, Robin, 107
Peyto, Wild Bill, 104-08
    appearance, 104
    behaviour, 104-06, 107-08
    Boer War, 106-07
    death, 108
    marriages, 107
    as park warden, 107
    Word War I, 107
phantom train, 230, 232
Philip, Prince, 5
Port aux Basques, Newfoundland, 96, 99, 101, 102
Port Hope, Ontario, 168-69
Prairie Pioneer Village and Museum, 34
Prohibition, 71-72

Q
Queensbury, Marquis of, 151

R
Rademuller, J.P., 225-28
    murder, 227
    War of 1812, 225
Rae, Sergeant William, 138
Red Saskatchewans see Fighting Fifth, Western Cavalry
Reffler, Fred, 93
Restall, Robert and Mildred, 121
Riel, Louis, 141, 145
Riley, Senator Dan, 63-65
Ripley's Believe It Or Not, 55, 203-04
Ritchie, H.B., 234
Roosevelt, Franklin D., 120
Ross, Hugo, 157
Ruth, Babe, 225

S

Sam Kee, 54-57
Sam Kee Building, 55
Seelye, Linus, 194-95
Selkirk, Lord, 144, 145
Sergeant Bill, 136-40
  promotion, 138
  restoration, 140
  World War I, 137-39
Shediac, New Brunswick, 24
Sheppard, Oliver, 214
Shum Moon, 55
Skottowe, Mabel, 82-83
Sladen, Dr. William, 8
Small, Ambrose, 211-16
  disappearance, 212
  marriage, 212-13
  parents, 213-14
Small, Daniel, 213
Small, Theresa, 212-13, 215-16
Smith, Captain Edward John, 156, 158,
  159
Smith, John, 117-19
Snodgrass, Reverend, 237-38, 240
Sontianen, 32-34
St. Ovide, Governor, 199-200
Standard Chemical Company, 156
Starkell, Dana, 88-92, 94-95
  asthma, 90, 95
Starkell, Don, 87-95
  Arctic voyage, 92-95
  in Brazil, 91-92
  childhood, 89
  in Colombia, 91
  frostbite, 95
  in Honduras, 90
  in Nicaragua, 91
  Paddle to the Amazon, 92
  Paddle to the Arctic, 95
Starkell, Jeff, 88-90, 95
Stevenson, Robert, 130-31, 132
Stone, Mrs. Winthrop, 106
Stoney First Nations, 61, 62, 63, 114
Sukanen, Tom, 29-34
  inventions, 31
  Sontianen, 32-34
  wife and children, 30, 31
Swanston, Vic, 139

T

The Three Truths, 79
Thompson, Franklin see Edmonds,
  Emma
Thompson, Harry, 232, 233
Through the Kalahari Desert, 167-68
Tilikum, 111-13
Tilikum, Luxton's Pacific Crossing, 115
Titanic, 154, 156-61
  hits iceberg, 157
Toronto Islands, 225
  lighthouse, 225, 227-28
Toronto Opera House, 214
train wreck, 232-33
Trask, Anne, 219-22
Trask, Charles, 221, 224
Triton Alliance, 121-22
Truro Company, 119
Twohey, Robert, 230-34
death prophecy, 231

U

Unsinkable Molly Brown see Brown,
  Margaret (Molly)

V

Vancouver, B.C., 55, 56
Vaughan, Anthony, 117-19
Victoria, B.C., 66-69
Voss, Captain John, 110-13

W

Wells, Ethel, 107-08
Wiarton, Ontario, 49
Wiarton Willie, 49-53
  death, 51, 53
  death threats, 50
  longevity, 53
Wilson, Edward Arthur see Brother
  Twelve
Wilson, Herbert, 83
Wilson, Tom, 106
Wood, Christina Adelaide, 133, 135
Wood, Emily, 107
Wray, Fay, 35

Y

Young, Joseph, 36-37